Original Title: MotoGP. Secrets and Legends

© MotoGP : Secrets and Legends, Carlos Martínez Cerdá and Víctor Martínez Cerdá, 2024.

Authors: Víctor Martínez Cerdá and Carlos Martínez Cerdá (V&C Brothers).

© Cover and Illustrations: V&C Brothers.

Layout and Design: V&C Brothers.

MOTOGP

SECRETS AND LEGENDS

1

The name "MotoGP" comes from the abbreviation of "Grand Prix Motorcycle Racing."

This championship is the premier class of the sport and brings together the 22 best riders in the world, divided into 11 teams.

The Motorcycle World Championship is held every year between March and November.

There are three categories: MotoGP, which is the premier class, as well as Moto2 and Moto3, which are the entry-level categories where younger riders take their first steps in the championship.

The MotoGP category stands out for using the most powerful and technologically advanced bikes, with 1000cc engines that can reach speeds of over 350 km/h.

Moto2 and Moto3, on the other hand, use less powerful engines, 765cc and 250cc respectively, and serve as development platforms for riders aiming to ascend to the main category.

The championship is contested on various circuits around the world, including iconic tracks like Mugello, Phillip Island, and the Circuit of the Americas.

The competition is managed by the International Motorcycling Federation (FIM) and is widely considered the pinnacle of motorcycle racing, attracting millions of viewers worldwide both on television and at the circuits.

2

Each MotoGP Grand Prix is held over three days and consists of three main parts: Free practice, qualifying sessions, and races.

Free practice allows riders to familiarize themselves with the circuit and adjust their bikes.

Several free practice sessions are held from Friday to Saturday.

The qualifying sessions determine the starting grid position for the race.

These sessions are divided into Q1 and Q2.

The 10 fastest riders from the free practice sessions advance directly to Q2, while the others compete in Q1.

The two fastest riders from Q1 advance to Q2, joining the 10 already qualified, for a total of 12 riders competing for pole position.

The grid positions are determined based on the times achieved in Q2.

The MotoGP race lasts approximately 45 minutes, during which the riders cover around 115 km.

On the grid, the riders line up in rows of three according to their qualifying times.

The points system in MotoGP is similar to that of Formula 1.

The first 15 riders to cross the finish line receive points, with 25 points for first place, 20 for second, 16 for third, and so on down to the fifteenth place, which receives 1 point.

At the end of the season, the rider with the most accumulated points is crowned world champion.

During practice, qualifying, and race sessions, riders must adhere to strict rules.

Failure to comply with these rules can result in penalties that may affect their qualifying position or even disqualify them from the race.

The races are held on various circuits around the world, each with unique characteristics that present different challenges to the riders and teams.

3

The MotoGP World Championship is contested with motorcycles equipped with 1000cc prototype engines that have a power output exceeding 270 horsepower.

These engines are specifically designed for top-level motorcycle racing and are not used in production motorcycles.

During races, the average speed is typically around 200 km/h, although this figure can vary depending on the circuit.

On the longest straights, MotoGP bikes can exceed 350 km/h, showcasing the impressive performance and capability of these machines.

This speed is remarkably high but still falls short of the absolute speed record on two wheels, which was set by Rocky Robinson.

Robinson reached a speed of 605.697 km/h with his streamliner, a motorcycle designed specifically to break straight-line speed records, putting into perspective the level of engineering and design required to achieve such extreme speeds.

MotoGP bikes are equipped with the latest technology in aerodynamics, advanced materials like carbon fiber, and sophisticated electronic systems including traction control, anti-lock braking systems (ABS), and real-time telemetry systems.

All of this combines to maximize performance and rider safety, requiring great skill and precision from the riders who handle these powerful machines.

The combination of high technology, rider skill, and team strategies makes MotoGP one of the most exciting and demanding competitions in the world of motorsport.

4

MotoGP riders extend their leg while braking for several reasons, although even among them, there isn't a clear consensus on the exact explanation.

This technique is not used to drag the foot on the ground to reduce speed, as one might initially think, but has other more complex and technical purposes.

Some theories include:

- Alteration of the physical behavior of the bike: Some riders believe that by extending the leg outward, the center of gravity and weight distribution of the bike is altered. This action can help stabilize the bike during hard braking and facilitate turning in corners. The extended leg acts like a compass, helping the bike follow a more precise trajectory when entering the corner.

- Improvement of stability: Another theory is that extending the leg offers an additional sense of stability and control. By having a part of their body outside the bike, riders can better feel the bike's reactions and adjust their posture and handling accordingly. This can be particularly useful in extreme braking situations where any additional information about the bike's behavior is valuable.

- Use as a "sensor": Some riders use their leg as a "sensor" to register the bike's reactions. By extending the leg, they can detect subtle changes in stability and tire grip, allowing them to adjust their riding technique in real time to avoid potential slides or loss of control.

- Reduction of pressure on the handlebars: Extending the leg can help reduce pressure on the handlebars, allowing riders to brake harder without compromising stability. By reducing the load on their arms and handlebars, riders can maintain more precise control of the steering.

5

They stick their knee out in the corners.

This technique allows riders to save time.

Firstly, it helps them "measure" the lean angle.

The contact between the track and the knee helps control the situation when the rear wheel loses grip.

By leaning the rider towards the inside of the turn, the bike has to lean less without losing any speed.

This technique, known as "hanging off," is crucial for maintaining stability and speed during corners.

Riders extend their knee to have a physical reference point that helps them evaluate and adjust their lean angle.

This allows them to maintain greater control over the bike and correct any potential slides.

By shifting their weight towards the inside of the turn, riders reduce the lean angle required for the bike, which improves grip and safety without sacrificing speed.

6

Can anyone become a MotoGP rider?

Becoming a MotoGP rider is not something that can be improvised, and the apparent ease with which they ride on the circuits is the result of years of hard work.

While some qualities are innate (talent is necessary), others, especially the physical ones, are gained through intensive training.

To master a bike that weighs 157 kg, has 270 horsepower, and reaches 350 km/h, one must be in perfect physical shape.

All MotoGP riders are elite athletes, although their preparation varies. While Aleix Espargaró does a lot of road cycling, the Frenchman Johann Zarco prefers climbing.

Riders must start from a very young age, often competing in lower categories such as Mini Motos, Moto3, and Moto2 before reaching MotoGP.

In addition to talent and skill on the track, riders need excellent physical condition to withstand the G-forces and physical stress of handling bikes at high speeds.

Training includes not only track practice but also cardiovascular, strength, and endurance exercises.

Mental preparation is also crucial, as riders must be able to concentrate intensely and make quick decisions under pressure.

Competing in MotoGP requires total commitment and dedication that goes beyond a passion for motorcycles; it is a combination of natural talent, rigorous training, and exceptional physical and mental discipline.

7

Superstitions of Riders.

1. Valentino Rossi: One of the most successful and charismatic riders in MotoGP, Rossi is known for his numerous pre-race rituals. Rossi always follows the same procedure before getting on the bike: he leans next to the bike, touches his boots, the grips, and the seat. Additionally, he always mounts the bike from the same side. Rossi has mentioned that these rituals help him concentrate and prepare his mind for the race.

2. Marc Márquez: He has the superstition of putting on his right glove before the left one and also putting on his right boot before the left one. Additionally, he has the habit of tapping the right footpeg of the bike several times with his right foot before starting the race.

3. Jorge Lorenzo: Before each race, Lorenzo performs a very detailed and meticulous physical warm-up. He is also known for being very precise with the placement of his gear, ensuring that everything is in its exact place.

4. Andrea Dovizioso: He has been seen performing small ritual gestures before each race, such as adjusting his helmet and gear in a specific way. These small rituals help many riders get into the "flow state" necessary to compete at the highest level.

5. Dani Pedrosa: He had the superstition of not allowing anyone to touch his helmet once he had placed it on his head before a race. He also performed certain repetitive movements to ensure he was completely prepared.

6. Nicky Hayden: The 2006 MotoGP world champion had the superstition of not cutting his hair during the racing season. He believed that keeping his hair the same way throughout the season brought him good luck.

7. Casey Stoner: The two-time MotoGP world champion had the superstition of not using the colors yellow and green together in his gear or on his bike. He believed that this color combination brought him bad luck.

8. Maverick Viñales: He has the habit of performing a concentration ritual before each race. He takes a moment to visualize the track and mentally prepare for the strategy he will use during the race.

9. Cal Crutchlow: Known for his straightforward personality and competitiveness, he has the superstition of not changing his gloves once he has used them during a practice session or a race. He believes that changing gloves could affect his performance.

10. Andrea Iannone: He is known for performing certain stretching and warm-up rituals in a specific sequence before getting on the bike. These rituals help him concentrate and prepare his body for the competition.

11. Alex Rins: He has the habit of lightly tapping the bike's stand with his foot before getting on it to start a race. He considers this gesture to bring him good luck and stability.

12. Johann Zarco: He performs a meditation and visualization ritual before each race. This ritual helps him calm down and focus on his race strategy. He also has the habit of touching certain points on the bike in a specific order before starting.

13. Álex Crivillé: The 1999 world champion used to walk around his bike before each race, always in a clockwise direction. This ritual helped him calm down and concentrate before the race.

14. Randy Mamola: A famous rider from the 80s, he used to wear the same pair of gloves throughout the season, believing they brought him good luck. Additionally, he always mounted the bike from the left side, considering it gave him a psychological advantage.

15. Kevin Schwantz: The 1993 world champion had the superstition of not allowing anyone to touch his bike once he had placed his helmet on the seat. He also used to cross himself before each race, asking for protection and luck.

16. Loris Capirossi: A MotoGP veteran, he had the habit of wearing the same socks throughout a race weekend if he had good results in practice or qualifying sessions. This small ritual gave him confidence for the races.

17. Marco Simoncelli: Known for his aggressive style and curly hair, he also had his rituals. One of them was always putting on his right glove before the left and ensuring his helmet was perfectly adjusted in a specific way before heading out onto the track.

18. Darryn Binder: The South African rider has the superstition of not allowing anyone to touch his helmet once he has placed it on his head. He also says a small prayer before each race, seeking peace and concentration.

19. Tito Rabat: He has the habit of tapping the handlebars three times before heading out onto the track, a ritual he has maintained since his Moto2 days that helps him feel connected with his bike.

20. Max Biaggi: Known as "The Roman Emperor," he had several superstitions. One of the most well-known was always putting on his helmet while on the bike before any session and not touching the bike before getting on it. Biaggi also had the habit of wearing the same underwear throughout a race weekend if he had good results in the initial sessions.

21. Franco Morbidelli: The Italian rider has the superstition of not talking too much about the race before competing. He prefers to stay calm and focused, avoiding discussions about strategies or possible results.

22. Pecco Bagnaia: He has a ritual where he must always enter the track with his right foot first. Additionally, he has the habit of touching the handlebars of his bike in a specific pattern before each race.

23. Fabio Quartararo: Known as "El Diablo," he has several pre-race rituals. He always puts on his left boot before the right and has a specific sequence for putting on his gloves and helmet. Additionally, he performs breathing exercises and visualization techniques to calm his nerves and mentally prepare.

24. Danilo Petrucci: He has the habit of giving three soft taps on the fuel tank of his bike before starting. He also always uses the same towel to dry his sweat during a race weekend, considering it a good luck charm.

25. Brad Binder: He has a ritual where he makes sure to touch his bike at certain points before each session. He believes this creates a special connection with the machine and gives him the confidence needed to compete.

26. Miguel Oliveira: The Portuguese rider has the superstition of not changing his helmet throughout a race weekend. He also performs a specific stretching routine before each session to ensure he is physically prepared.

27. Takaaki Nakagami: He always mounts the bike from the left side and has the habit of lightly tapping the footpegs with his boots before heading onto the track. Additionally, he carries a small lucky charm given to him by a fan.

28. Joan Mir: The 2020 world champion has the habit of lightly tapping the handlebars of his bike with his gloves before starting a race. He also tends to repeat certain motivational phrases in his mind to stay focused and confident.

29. Jack Miller: He is known for his habit of biting the strap of his helmet before each race. He believes this ritual helps him stay calm and focused. Additionally, he always takes a small jump before getting on the bike, a habit he has maintained since his Moto3 days.

8

MotoGP has its roots in the World Motorcycle Championship, which was established in 1949 by the International Motorcycling Federation (FIM).

This championship is considered the oldest in motorcycle racing competitions and has been the pinnacle of the two-wheeled sport since its inception.

The origins of competitive motorcycling date back to the early 20th century, with races organized on roads and circuits in Europe.

In particular, the races on the Isle of Man, known as the Tourist Trophy (TT), were some of the first to gain notoriety.

These races began in 1907 and quickly became a benchmark in the motorcycling world.

The 1949 World Motorcycle Championship included several categories based on engine size: 125cc, 250cc, 350cc, and 500cc, as well as a sidecar category.

The 500cc category, which would later become MotoGP, was the premier class from the start.

The motorcycles used in these early competitions were modified production models, but over time, bikes were developed specifically for competing in the championship.

In the 1950s and 1960s, brands like MV Agusta, Norton, and Moto Guzzi dominated the races.

Giacomo Agostini, a rider for MV Agusta, became a legend in the sport, winning 15 world titles throughout his career.

In these years, technology and racing tactics evolved rapidly, and the bikes became faster and more sophisticated.

The 1970s saw a significant shift with the introduction of Japanese motorcycles from manufacturers like Honda, Yamaha, Suzuki, and Kawasaki.

These brands began to dominate the championship, bringing technological advancements and fierce competition.

In 1978, Kenny Roberts, an American Yamaha rider, revolutionized riding style by introducing the "hanging off" technique, which is now common in motorcycle racing.

In 2002, the 500cc championship was renamed MotoGP, and the use of four-stroke engines with a limit of 990cc was allowed, replacing the traditional 500cc two-stroke engines.

This transition marked the beginning of a new era in the sport, with greater emphasis on advanced technology and electronics in the bikes.

In 2007, the displacement limit was reduced to 800cc to improve safety, and in 2012, it was increased to the current 1000cc.

MotoGP has continued to evolve, with changes in technical regulations to promote safety and fair competition.

The series has also expanded its race calendar globally, visiting circuits on every continent and attracting a worldwide audience.

9

Example of a Training Day.

1. Cardiovascular Exercise (6:00 a.m. - 7:30 a.m.):
- **Running or Cycling:** Many riders prefer road cycling, like Aleix Espargaró, who engages in long sessions to improve cardiovascular endurance. Alternatively, they may do long-distance runs or interval training to enhance aerobic and anaerobic capacity.

2. Breakfast and Rest (7:30 a.m. - 9:00 a.m.):
- **Nutritious Breakfast:** A mix of proteins, complex carbohydrates, and healthy fats. Examples include eggs, oatmeal, fruits, and nuts.
- **Rest:** Time for recovery and preparation for the next training session.

3. Strength and Core Training (9:30 a.m. - 11:00 a.m.):
- **Weightlifting:** Includes exercises like bench press, squats, deadlifts, and Olympic lifts to increase strength and power.
- **Core Training:** Exercises such as planks, crunches, and stability workouts to strengthen the core, which is crucial for bike control.

4. Lunch and Rest (11:30 a.m. - 1:00 p.m.):
- **Balanced Lunch:** Rich in lean proteins (chicken, fish), carbohydrates (brown rice, pasta), and vegetables.
- **Short Nap:** 30-45 minutes of rest to recharge energy.

5. On-Bike Training (2:00 p.m. - 4:00 p.m.):
- **Track Practice:** When possible, riders perform sessions on the bike to practice specific techniques, such as braking, acceleration, and cornering.
- **Simulators:** If they don't have access to the track, they use high-tech simulators to train reflexes and race strategies.

6. Technical Training (4:30 p.m. - 6:00 p.m.):
- **Gym Work:** Focus on high-intensity and functional exercises to improve endurance and agility.
- **Flexibility Training:** Yoga or deep stretching to improve flexibility and prevent injuries.

7. Dinner and Recovery (6:30 p.m. - 8:00 p.m.):
- **Nutritious Dinner:** Rich in proteins and carbohydrates for muscle recovery.
- **Ice Baths or Recovery Therapy:** To reduce inflammation and speed up muscle recovery.
- **Stretching and Relaxation:** Stretching routines and relaxation techniques to help the body recover.

8. Night Rest (10:00 p.m.):
- **Restorative Sleep:** At least 8 hours of sleep for optimal recovery. Riders may also use meditation or mindfulness techniques to improve sleep quality and mental recovery.

10

Andrea Iannone, an Italian MotoGP rider, achieved an impressive record in the world of motorcycling.

This milestone took place at the Qatar Grand Prix in 2016, where on the longest straight of the Losail circuit, Iannone managed to reach a speed of 354.9 kilometers per hour.

This achievement surpassed previous historical records, including that of Marc Márquez, who had reached a speed of 350.5 km/h at the same circuit.

Iannone, born on August 9, 1989, in Vasto, Italy, has had a notable career in MotoGP, known for his speed and aggressive riding style.

He began his career in the lower categories, competing in the 125cc World Championship and then in Moto2, before making his debut in the premier MotoGP category in 2013 with the Pramac Racing team.

Iannone's speed record still stands in MotoGP history, highlighting one of the most impressive feats in the modern era of motorcycling.

His achievement in Qatar not only demonstrates his skill as a rider but also the advanced technical development of MotoGP bikes, capable of reaching extreme speeds while maintaining a high level of control and safety.

Despite his success on the track, Iannone's career has also faced challenges.

In 2019, he was temporarily suspended due to a doping rule violation, which has affected his career since then.

Despite these setbacks, his speed record remains a testament to his talent and contribution to the sport.

11

Marc Márquez, the seven-time MotoGP world champion, is known not only for his number 93 but also for his distinctive symbol: an ant.

The reason behind this symbol dates back to the early days of his professional motorcycle racing career.

When Márquez began competing professionally, his body weight was considerably low for the demands of the sport.

This presented a significant challenge as racing motorcycles require a certain weight balance to handle properly.

To compensate for his light weight, his team had to overload the motorcycle with an additional 21 kilograms.

This adaptation was crucial for Márquez to compete on equal terms with his rivals.

The choice of the ant as his symbol is directly connected to this experience.

Ants are known for their ability to carry weights many times their own body weight.

Similarly, Márquez had to compete for several years with an additional load that doubled his own weight, a true feat of endurance and skill.

This similarity with ants, which can carry up to 50 times their body weight, made the ant a perfect symbol to represent Márquez's tenacity and strength on the track.

The nickname and symbol of the ant have become an integral part of Márquez's identity, reflecting his determination and ability to overcome physical obstacles throughout his career.

12

In 2017, MotoGP recorded a historic number of crashes, making it the year with the most accidents in the championship's history.

During that season, a total of 313 crashes were recorded among all the riders, a figure that had never been reached before.

The crashes occurred in the three main categories of the championship: MotoGP, Moto2, and Moto3.

This high incidence of accidents was due to several factors, including adverse weather conditions in some races, extreme competitiveness among the riders, and the technical characteristics of the tracks.

One of the most notable circuits in terms of crashes was the Spanish Grand Prix in Jerez, where there was a significant number of accidents.

Additionally, other circuits like Valencia and Phillip Island also witnessed numerous crashes.

The increase in the number of crashes in 2017 also highlighted the importance of safety in the sport.

Organizers and teams have continuously worked to improve safety measures, both on the tracks and in the riders' equipment, to reduce the risk of serious injuries.

Among the riders who experienced crashes that year were some of the sport's most prominent names, including Marc Márquez, Andrea Dovizioso, Cal Crutchlow, Jorge Lorenzo, and Dani Pedrosa.

13

The Jerez circuit, officially known as the Circuito de Jerez-Ángel Nieto, has a total of 13 corners, but it is often referred to as "12+1" in commemoration of Ángel Nieto.

Ángel Nieto, a legend of Spanish motorcycling, won 13 world titles during his career, but due to his superstition, he avoided mentioning the number 13, referring to his titles as "12+1."

This superstition of Nieto is also reflected in the circuit that bears his name.

Nieto is considered one of the most successful and beloved riders in the history of Spanish and world motorcycling.

His aversion to the number 13 was well known in the sports world, and as a sign of respect and in honor of his achievements, the Jerez circuit adopted the reference "12+1" for the corners.

In 2017, after the death of Ángel Nieto, the Jerez circuit was officially renamed in his honor, becoming the Circuito de Jerez-Ángel Nieto.

This decision was a way to perpetuate his legacy and his contribution to the world of motorcycling.

The Circuito de Jerez is one of the most important and iconic circuits on the MotoGP calendar and has hosted numerous memorable races since its inauguration in 1985.

14

Losail, the most demanding circuit, is located in the northeast of Qatar and has a length of 5.400 meters, consisting of 16 corners.

The most notable feature of this circuit is that it is the only one on the MotoGP calendar that takes place entirely at night.

The main reason for this is that during the day, the track temperature can reach 45 degrees Celsius, making it unsuitable for both riders and machines.

The construction of the Losail circuit was completed in record time, delivered in less than a year (10 months).

More than 1,000 people worked on the project to ensure everything was ready for its inauguration.

The track was evaluated by the MotoGP Safety Commission, which includes prominent riders such as Valentino Rossi, Sete Gibernau, Kenny Roberts Jr., and Nobuatsu Aoki, who supervised and ensured that the track met the necessary safety standards for high-speed competitions.

The Losail circuit is known not only for its night races but also for its technical complexity.

The 16 corners, combined with artificial lighting, present a unique challenge for both riders and teams.

The night races at Losail are an impressive visual spectacle and require a different approach in terms of race strategy and bike setup due to the temperature variations between day and night.

The lighting installation at Losail is one of the largest in the world for a sports circuit, allowing races to be held in optimal lighting conditions.

15

Famous Quotes from MotoGP Riders.

1. Valentino Rossi:
- "Speed is not about killing time, but about enjoying every second."
- "Winning in MotoGP is a great pleasure, but the greatest pleasure is riding a motorcycle."

2. Marc Márquez:
- "When the opportunity arises, you cannot let it pass."
- "The key to success is to stay calm in difficult moments and enjoy the good ones."

3. Jorge Lorenzo:
- "The bike is like a lover; you have to know it well to get the most out of it."
- "Talent gives you an advantage, but hard work and dedication are what really make the difference."

4. Casey Stoner:
- "Racing is all I've known since I was a kid. It's my life."
- "I don't race for fame or money; I race because I love racing."

5. Nicky Hayden:
- "Never give up, no matter how tough things get."
- "Champions aren't made in the gyms; they are made of something they have deep inside them: a desire, a dream, a vision."

6. Dani Pedrosa:
- "Every time I get on the bike, I forget everything else."
- "Motorcycling is a sport of passion; every rider has a fire inside that pushes them forward."

7. Kevin Schwantz:
- "Race every lap like it's your last."
- "Speed is relative. If you feel comfortable, you're not going fast enough."

8. Mick Doohan:
- "To be the best, you have to beat the best, and that's exactly what I aim to do."
- "The key to being fast is always being one step ahead of the rest."

9. Andrea Dovizioso:
- "To be competitive in MotoGP, you need to have a strong mind and be willing to push your limits."
- "The key to success is learning from every mistake and not being defeated by them."

10. Ángel Nieto:
- "My life is the bike. I don't know how to do anything else."
- "Winning is not the most important thing; it's the only thing."

11. Giacomo Agostini:
- "Speed makes me feel free and alive."
- "Racing motorcycles is a passion that cannot be described with words."

12. Wayne Rainey:
- "Motorcycling is a sport where there is no room for error."
- "Every race is a new opportunity to prove your worth."

13. Freddie Spencer:
- "To be fast on a bike, you need to have confidence in yourself and your machine."
- "Mental preparation is as important as physical preparation."

14. Loris Capirossi:
- "Every time I get on the bike, I feel a mix of fear and excitement."
- "Motorcycling is a sport of bravery and precision."

15. Alex Crivillé:
- "Winning in MotoGP is a dream come true."
- "The passion for motorcycles is something
you carry within you from childhood."

16. Kenny Roberts Sr.:
- "The only way to be the best is never to be satisfied
with being good."
- "Speed is addictive, and adrenaline is what drives us."

17. Randy Mamola:
- "Motorcycling is not just a sport; it's a way of life."
- "The key to being a good rider is never underestimating
the power of fear."

18. Marco Simoncelli:
- "The adrenaline you feel on the track is incomparable
to anything else in life."
- "Racing motorcycles is a constant battle against yourself
and your own limits."

19. Barry Sheene:
- "Races are won or lost in the head, not on the track."
- "To be fast on a bike, you need the courage of a lion
and the agility of a cat."

20. Jack Miller:
- "Speed is my drug, and the bike is my escape."
- "Every race is an opportunity to show what you're
made of."

21. Miguel Oliveira:
- "It's not just about winning; it's about improving
every day."
- "Motorcycling is a sport of precision and passion."

22. Cal Crutchlow:
- "Never underestimate the power of determination
and hard work."
- "The bike doesn't make the rider; the rider makes
the bike."

16

Controversies Involving Famous Riders.

1. Valentino Rossi and the 2015 Sepang Incident:
At the 2015 Malaysian Grand Prix, Valentino Rossi and Marc Márquez were involved in one of the most controversial incidents in recent MotoGP history. Rossi was accused of deliberately causing Márquez to crash during the race, which led to Rossi being penalized and forced to start from the last position in the following race, which was crucial for the championship. Although not a cheat in the strict sense, the incident was perceived as unsportsmanlike by many.

2. Marc Márquez and Accusations of Interference:
During the same 2015 season, Marc Márquez was accused of interfering in the championship battle between Valentino Rossi and Jorge Lorenzo. Rossi suggested that Márquez was intentionally helping Lorenzo by slowing him down in some races, which generated significant controversy in the paddock. These accusations were never proven.

3. Andrea Iannone and Doping Suspension:
In December 2019, Andrea Iannone was provisionally suspended by the FIM after testing positive for a banned substance during the Malaysian Grand Prix. He was later sanctioned with an 18-month suspension, which was extended to four years after an appeal. Iannone has always maintained his innocence, arguing that the positive result was due to food contamination.

4. Valentino Rossi and Alleged Use of Illegal Fuel in 2003:
In 2003, when Rossi was racing for Honda, there were rumors that his team was using fuel that did not comply with MotoGP regulations. However, these accusations were never proven.

5. John Hopkins and Bike Weight:
Hopkins was accused several times of racing with a bike that did not meet the minimum weight requirements. These rumors arose due to his impressive straight-line speed, but no concrete evidence was ever found to sanction him.

6. Casey Stoner and Accusations of Illegal Electronics:

During the 2007 season, there were rumors that Ducati, Casey Stoner's team, was using illegal electronics on his bike to improve performance. These accusations were never proven, but they generated much discussion in the paddock due to Stoner's dominance that year, in which he won his first world championship.

7. Dani Pedrosa and the Honda Chassis Controversy:

In 2013, it was suspected that Honda had developed a special chassis for Dani Pedrosa that did not comply with MotoGP regulations. Although there was no conclusive evidence, the incident highlighted the differences in treatment of riders within the same team.

8. Michael Doohan and Alleged Use of Traction Control:

In the 90s, when Mick Doohan was dominating the premier class with Honda, there were speculations about the use of an illegal traction control system on his bike. These accusations were never confirmed, but they persisted due to the notable advantage Doohan had over his competitors.

9. Kenny Roberts Jr. and Alleged Use of Illegal Tires:

During the 2000 season, Kenny Roberts Jr. was accused of using illegal tires that provided an unfair advantage in terms of traction and durability. Although there was not enough evidence to sanction him, the suspicions affected the perception of his victories.

10. Valentino Rossi and the Incident with Sete Gibernau in 2005:

At the 2005 Jerez Grand Prix, Valentino Rossi and Sete Gibernau were involved in a controversial race finish. Rossi made an aggressive move in the final corner, resulting in contact that forced Gibernau off the track, allowing Rossi to win the race. Although not a cheat in the strict sense, the maneuver was seen by many as unsportsmanlike.

11. Maverick Viñales and Fuel Irregularity Accusations:

In 2016, during his time with Suzuki, Maverick Viñales was the subject of rumors about using fuel that did not comply with regulatory specifications. These accusations were never proven, but they created an atmosphere of suspicion around the team.

12. Aleix Espargaró and the Use of Illegal Engine Maps:

On several occasions, Aleix Espargaró has been accused of using engine maps that did not comply with MotoGP regulations, giving him an advantage in certain race conditions. Although these accusations did not lead to formal sanctions, they added tension to the competitions.

13. Álex Debón and Flag Violations in 2008:

During the 2008 Portuguese Grand Prix in the 250cc category, Álex Debón was penalized for ignoring yellow flags indicating danger on the track. This resulted in a time penalty that affected his final position in the race.

14. Sete Gibernau and the Tire Controversy in 2004:

In 2004, Sete Gibernau was accused of using tires that did not meet technical specifications during the Qatar Grand Prix. Although the team denied the accusations, this incident generated much controversy and discussions about fairness in competitions.

15. Loris Capirossi and Accusations of Using Modified Brakes:

In the mid-2000s, there were rumors that Loris Capirossi was using illegally modified brakes to gain an advantage in braking. These accusations were never proven, but they created suspicions and tensions in the paddock.

16. Colin Edwards and the Bike Weight Controversy:

Colin Edwards was accused several times of racing with a bike that did not meet the minimum weight regulations. Although conclusive evidence was never found, these rumors affected the perception of his performances in some races.

17. Makoto Tamada and the Use of Fuel Additives:

During the 2004 season, Makoto Tamada was suspected of using illegal additives in the fuel to improve his bike's performance. Despite the suspicions, there was not enough evidence to sanction him.

18. Max Biaggi and Accusations of Bike Tampering:

Max Biaggi, known for his intense rivalry with Valentino Rossi, was accused several times of illegally tampering with his bike to gain a competitive advantage. These accusations were never confirmed, but they contributed to the tension between teams and riders.

17

**A MotoGP bike is capable of accelerating
from 0 to 100 km/h in just 2.5 seconds.**

This figure is impressive and reflects the incredible
power and efficiency of these racing machines.

To put this in perspective, if we compare this acceleration
with that of a Formula 1 car, we find that a Formula 1 car
can accelerate from 0 to 100 km/h in approximately 2.8
seconds.

Although Formula 1 cars are known for their speed
and advanced technology, MotoGP bikes have a slight
advantage in this aspect due to their lower weight and
high performance.

Additionally, if we compare a MotoGP bike with a
superbike like the Kawasaki H2R, which is considered
one of the fastest production motorcycles in the world,
the Kawasaki H2R also accelerates from 0 to 100 km/h
in around 2.8 seconds.

The MotoGP bike even surpasses this motorcycle,
highlighting its superiority in terms of acceleration.

**The rapid acceleration of the bikes is due to several
factors:**

- **Lightweight:** MotoGP bikes have a minimum weight of
around 157 kg, making them much lighter than a Formula
1 car, which weighs approximately 752 kg without fuel or
driver. This weight difference significantly contributes to
their acceleration capability.

- Engine Power: MotoGP bikes are equipped with 1000 cc engines that can produce more than 270 horsepower, providing an extremely high power-to-weight ratio.

- Advanced Technology: MotoGP bikes use advanced technologies such as traction control, carbon brake systems, and electronic suspensions, which help maximize efficiency and traction during acceleration.

- Aerodynamic Design: Although less aerodynamic than Formula 1 cars, MotoGP bikes are designed to minimize wind resistance and maximize stability at high speeds.

- Specialized Tires: The tires used in MotoGP are specifically designed to provide maximum traction and grip, which is crucial for achieving rapid acceleration.

18

The engines of MotoGP bikes operate at an impressive maximum performance, regularly reaching the rev limiter at 18,000 rpm.

This figure is extraordinarily high, especially when compared to other high-performance vehicles.

For example, the Kawasaki H2R, one of the fastest and most powerful superbikes in the world, has a maximum rev limit of 14,000 rpm.

The ability of MotoGP engines to reach and maintain such high revolutions is due to a combination of advanced engineering and design factors.

The internal components of the engines, such as pistons, connecting rods, and valves, are made from lightweight and extremely durable materials like titanium alloys and carbon fiber.

These materials can withstand the high temperatures and stress generated at 18,000 rpm.

Additionally, MotoGP engines use pneumatic valve systems instead of traditional spring systems, which allow for more precise control of the valves at high revs, reducing the possibility of mechanical failure and improving engine efficiency.

At 18,000 rpm, friction and heat are enormous challenges.

MotoGP engines feature advanced lubrication and cooling systems that ensure the engine stays within proper operating temperatures, preventing overheating and premature wear.

The design of MotoGP engines is specifically optimized to maximize power and revolutions per minute, including cylinder configuration and combustion optimization to achieve maximum performance.

The electronic systems in MotoGP bikes play a crucial role.

Traction control, engine mapping, and other electronic systems help manage power delivery and keep the engine running efficiently and safely at high revs.

Additionally, MotoGP manufacturers constantly invest in research and development to improve the performance of their engines.

This includes bench testing and simulations that allow continuous adjustment and improvement of the engines.

The fact that MotoGP engines can regularly reach and maintain 18,000 rpm not only demonstrates the level of engineering and technology applied but also the extreme robustness and reliability required in high-competition racing.

19

**The engines of these motorcycles allow
the intake of 150 liters of air per second.**

This is equivalent to breathing 25 times per second.

This enormous amount of air directly influences the amount
of power and horsepower the bike can generate.

The operation of a MotoGP engine is based on a precise
combination of air and fuel.

At high revolutions, like those reached by MotoGP bikes,
which can go up to 18,000 rpm, the demand for air is immense
to maintain combustion efficiency and maximize engine power.

The air intake systems are designed to optimize airflow into
the engine, ensuring an ideal air-fuel mixture at all times.

The air enters through the intake ducts and passes through
the air filter before mixing with the fuel in the injectors.

This mixture is compressed in the cylinders and ignited
by spark plugs, producing the combustion that generates
the necessary power to propel the bike.

The efficiency of this process is crucial for the bike's
performance, as any restriction in the airflow can reduce
power and overall performance.

The management of this airflow is facilitated by advanced
electronic systems that constantly monitor and adjust the
amount of air and fuel entering the engine.

These systems allow for a quick and precise response
to changing driving conditions, ensuring that the engine
operates optimally at all times.

20

**Not only are the bikes strong;
the riders must be as well.**

A MotoGP rider is capable of enduring braking
forces of up to 1.5G on their arms.

This means that when braking, a rider experiences
a force equivalent to having the weight of a person
of about 50-60 kg pushing forward at 350 km/h.

This ability to withstand such extreme forces
requires intense physical and mental preparation.

MotoGP riders have exhaustive training routines that
include endurance, strength, and flexibility exercises.

Cardiovascular training is crucial to maintain
endurance during long and demanding races.

Additionally, strength exercises, especially in the
upper body and core, are essential to withstand
the G-forces during braking and acceleration.

During a race, riders experience G-forces in various
directions: forward during braking, backward during
acceleration, and laterally during cornering.

The 1.5G force during braking means that the bike
and rider must withstand a great deceleration in
a short period, which is extremely physically
demanding.

In addition to braking, corners also generate significant lateral forces that riders must counteract through their posture and control over the bike.

The equipment, such as racing suits and helmets, is also designed to help riders manage these forces.

The suits are tight-fitting and aerodynamic, providing additional support and minimizing air resistance.

The helmets are lightweight yet extremely strong, protecting the rider's head while withstanding G-forces.

Nutrition and recovery are equally important.

Riders follow strict diets designed to maintain their weight at optimal levels and provide the necessary energy for their intense training sessions and races.

Recovery includes physiotherapy, massages, and other techniques to ensure their bodies recover quickly from the physical demands.

21

The anatomy of MotoGP suits is crucial to ensure the safety of riders who drive at speeds exceeding 300 kilometers per hour.

These suits, also known as leathers, are a key element in protecting motorcyclists, as they must balance two crucial characteristics: freedom of movement and extreme durability.

MotoGP riders use several protective elements, including gloves, elbow pads, back protectors, knee pads, boots, and helmets; however, the suit is the most extensive and essential component of their protective gear.

The suits are designed to keep all protections in place during a crash and to withstand the abrasion of impact without being completely destroyed.

A MotoGP suit weighs approximately 4.5 kilograms and is usually made of cowhide or sometimes kangaroo leather.

This material not only provides durability but also offers the necessary flexibility for the rider to move freely.

In addition to durability, the suits must keep riders cool, so they feature an integrated ventilation system.

Air enters through small holes in the front of the suit, circulates inside, and exits through holes in the back, helping to keep the rider comfortable during the race.

An advanced feature of these suits is the built-in airbag system.

This system automatically activates in the event of a crash, providing vital protection for the rider's ribs, torso, and collarbones.

The airbag functions like a vest that inflates, allowing the suit to expand by 4 to 5 centimeters in the areas where the airbags are located.

The airbag is connected to precisely calibrated gyroscopes and accelerometers, ensuring it only deploys in actual crashes and not at speeds below approximately 25 km/h.

The speed of this system is impressive: while a human blink lasts around 350 milliseconds, the airbag deploys in just 25 milliseconds, providing immediate and effective protection for the rider.

22

**Being a MotoGP rider means dealing
with a lot of heat.**

Racing in an ambient temperature of 35 degrees, inside a leather suit, and controlling a 150-kilogram motorcycle at over 300 km/h is thrilling but also very hot.

During a race, the combination of high speed, physical exertion, and extreme weather conditions can lead to significant fluid loss through sweating.

By the end of a MotoGP race, a rider can lose between 2 and 3% of their body weight, which equals 1.5 to 2 kilograms of pure sweat.

The high temperature inside the leather suit, which is designed to protect the rider in case of a fall, adds an additional challenge.

These suits, although equipped with integrated ventilation systems, can still become virtual ovens under the heat of the asphalt and the intense physical activity required to handle the motorcycle at such speeds.

The combination of ambient heat, the heat generated by the rider's body, and the heat produced by the bike makes the experience extremely exhausting.

For this reason, hydration becomes a key aspect of a MotoGP rider's performance.

Dehydration can quickly affect a rider's concentration and reaction time, which is crucial in a competition where every millisecond counts.

A dehydrated rider is more prone to making mistakes, which can be dangerous both for themselves and for other competitors on the track.

23

The Japanese are unbeatable.

As in Formula One, each MotoGP season includes two distinct championships: one for riders and one for teams.

The Team World Championship is won by the team that accumulates the most successes during the season, based on the points their riders earn in each of the Grand Prix races.

It is worth mentioning that it is possible for the MotoGP champion rider not to belong to the champion team.

Since 2002, when the new era began under the name MotoGP, there have been 19 championships, and 18 of them were won by Japanese teams.

Only in 2007 did the Ducati Marlboro Team break this streak and bring the trophy to Italy.

Interestingly, since the first championship in 1949, no Japanese rider has ever won a championship.

In contrast, Italian riders have been the most successful, with 20 world titles, followed by those from the United Kingdom.

And while we are mentioning curiosities about the champions, there was once a champion from Southern Rhodesia.

This peculiarity highlights the dominance of Japanese teams in the team category, while individual riders from Japan have yet to achieve the title of world champion in the history of MotoGP.

24

The bikes in the premier class, known as MotoGP, represent the pinnacle of technology in the world of motorcycling.

These machines are equipped with more than 40 different sensors that measure a wide range of critical parameters for performance and safety.

Among the data collected are pressures, forces, speeds, temperatures, and vibrations, among others.

During a Grand Prix weekend, each MotoGP bike can gather approximately 30 GB of data.

This massive data collection is essential for analyzing and adjusting the performance of the bikes.

Engineers and technicians use this data to understand the bike's behavior under different conditions and make adjustments to improve its performance.

However, unlike other motorsports like Formula One and the Red Bull Air Race, MotoGP does not allow the use of real-time telemetry.

In Formula One, the cars are constantly sending data to their teams, who analyze it in real time to make immediate decisions that can influence the course of the race.

The same is true in the Red Bull Air Race, where planes constantly transmit information.

In MotoGP, regulations prohibit this practice.

The information collected during practice, qualifying, and race sessions is stored locally on a hard drive within the bike.

This information can only be downloaded at the end of the day, and the process is done via a cable connection.

This means that any adjustments based on the data collected during a race must wait until the information can be analyzed after the session.

This restriction implies that MotoGP teams must rely on post-race analysis to make adjustments and improvements, adding an extra layer of challenge and strategy compared to other motorsports where real-time telemetry is a fundamental tool.

The absence of real-time telemetry forces the riders and teams to be more intuitive and reactive during the race, making the skill and experience of the riders even more crucial.

25

The invention of the mobile clinic is a significant milestone in the history of the Motorcycle World Championship, also known as MotoGP.

Given the extreme and highly competitive nature of this sport, riders are constantly pushing the limits, which inevitably leads to a high number of crashes and accidents each season.

The safety of the riders is, therefore, a primary concern.

In order to provide immediate and effective medical care to injured riders, the Motorcycle World Championship introduced a professionalized mobile clinic at the circuits in 1977.

This revolutionary initiative radically changed the way medical emergencies were handled during races.

The mobile clinic is equipped with advanced medical equipment and specialized personnel, capable of providing immediate care at the site of the accident.

The implementation of the mobile clinic has had a profound and positive impact on rider safety.

By being able to receive medical attention quickly after a crash, a large number of lives have been saved, and the severity of many injuries has been reduced.

The mobile clinic acts as an emergency room on wheels, with the capability to perform immediate diagnostics and treatments, stabilizing riders before they are transferred to larger medical facilities if necessary.

The success of this measure in the Motorcycle World Championship did not go unnoticed by other major motor racing competitions.

The efficiency and benefits of having a mobile clinic at the circuits led to this practice being adopted by other motorsport disciplines.

Formula One races, rally competitions, and many other motorsport series have followed suit, establishing their own mobile clinics to improve competitor safety.

The mobile clinic has not only enhanced rider safety during races but has also advanced the development of specific medical protocols for treating common injuries in motorsports.

The experience accumulated over the years has allowed for the refinement of on-track medical care techniques, making the sport safer and reducing the recovery time for riders after accidents.

26

In the Motorcycle World Championship, crashes are an inevitable aspect due to the competitive and extreme nature of the sport.

Each year, more than 1,000 crashes are recorded during the season.

The average over the past few years confirms this trend, reflecting the high risk and skill level required to compete in these categories.

The record for crashes in a single season was reached in 2017, with a total of 1,126 crashes.

This number is broken down into the three main categories of the championship: Moto2, Moto3, and MotoGP.

In that season, Moto2 had the highest number of incidents with 434 crashes.

This category is known for its high level of competitiveness and the use of bikes with specific characteristics that can contribute to a higher incidence of crashes.

Moto3, the entry-level category where young talents compete, recorded 379 crashes.

Despite having less powerful bikes compared to Moto2 and MotoGP, the intensity of the races and the close proximity of the riders on the track increase the risk of accidents.

In MotoGP, the premier class of motorcycling, there were 313 crashes in 2017.

Although this number is lower compared to Moto2 and Moto3, the higher speeds and technical complexity of MotoGP bikes mean that each crash has the potential to be more severe.

The high number of crashes in all categories of the Motorcycle World Championship reflects the commitment and bravery of the riders, who constantly push the limits to win.

27

The 1969 Isle of Man Tourist Trophy (TT) holds the record for the highest number of participants in a single race, with a total of 97 riders competing in the 500cc category.

This historic race is one of the most iconic and challenging events in the world of motorcycling, known for its dangerous and demanding course through the public roads of the island.

The 1969 edition of the Isle of Man TT was especially notable not only for the record number of participants but also for the level of competition and talent present in the race.

Giacomo Agostini, one of the most legendary riders in motorcycling history, won this race.

Agostini is widely recognized for his impressive achievements, including eight World Championship titles in the 500cc category, cementing his status as one of the greatest riders of all time.

The 1969 race stood out for its complexity and the skill required to compete in it.

The Isle of Man TT circuit is known for its long distances, abrupt elevation changes, tight corners, and the lack of modern safety measures found on closed racing circuits.

These factors make the TT an extreme challenge, where the riders' skill, concentration, and courage are tested at every moment.

Agostini's success in the 1969 TT is a testament to his exceptional skill and mastery in motorcycling.

Winning an event with so many participants on such a dangerous circuit highlights his talent and determination.

Moreover, his victory contributed to his legacy in the sport, enhancing his reputation and leaving an indelible mark on the history of motorcycling.

28

**Hermann Tilke is a German engineer
and architect who has gained worldwide
renown for his race track designs.**

Throughout his career, he has designed around
70 circuits globally, noted for his ability to balance
safety and spectacle in his layouts.

Some of his most recognized designs include circuits
like Sepang (Malaysia), Circuit of the Americas
(USA), Motorland Aragón (Spain), Sachsenring
(Germany), Yas Marina (Abu Dhabi), Bahrain
International Circuit, Istanbul Park (Turkey),
as well as urban circuits in cities like Bucharest,
Hanoi, and New York.

Tilke has been a key figure in the modernization
of Formula 1 circuits and other motor racing
competitions, but his designs have not been
without criticism.

One of the main critiques is that his circuits
often look too similar to each other and offer few
overtaking opportunities, which can reduce the
excitement and unpredictability of the races.

In response to these criticisms, Tilke has defended
his designs by arguing that the extensive asphalt
run-off areas are essential to protect both
professional drivers and amateurs who
participatein events with their own vehicles.

These run-off areas help reduce the severity of accidents by providing a safe space for vehicles to decelerate off the track.

The process of designing a race circuit is extremely complex and goes far beyond the initial layout.

Among the many factors that must be considered are driver safety, run-off zones, spectator locations, and the circuit's adaptability for different types of tests and events.

A circuit is not just a place to enjoy motorsport; it also needs to be a profitable and versatile business.

The Circuit de Barcelona-Catalunya, commonly known as Montmeló, is a perfect example of this versatility.

This circuit is active almost every day of the year, hosting a variety of events ranging from high-level competitions to track days for enthusiasts and vehicle testing.

This ensures a constant flow of revenue and keeps the circuit in continuous use, demonstrating how good design can balance the passion for motorsport with economic viability.

29

Jarno Zaffelli is a prominent Italian circuit designer specializing in motorcycle rider safety.

His reputation in the industry is largely due to his innovative approach to improving safety on race tracks.

One of his most notable creations is the DroCAS simulator, an advanced tool that allows for the analysis of risks faced by motorcyclists on different layouts.

DroCAS uses data and simulations to identify and mitigate potential hazards on circuits, helping to design safer and more efficient tracks.

Due to his expertise and knowledge in safety, Zaffelli is a trusted expert in the Motorcycle World Championship for circuit updates.

One of his recent projects includes the renovation of the Silverstone circuit, where he was hired for the resurfacing of the track.

This task is crucial to ensure that the circuit meets the highest standards of safety and performance, especially on such an iconic and frequently used track.

In Spain, we have circuit design experts like Jaume Nogué.

With extensive experience in the industry, Nogué has designed a dozen national and international tracks.

Among his projects are well-known circuits like Montmeló, Navarra, Bilbao, Huesca, and Valencia.

His work also extends to countries such as Argentina, Russia, and Mauritius.

Jaume Nogué, in addition to being an engineer, is a former amateur racer, which gives him a unique perspective on circuit design.

He imagines racing on each track he designs to ensure they meet the highest standards of quality and safety.

This practice of visualizing and personally testing the circuits both by car and motorcycle allows Nogué to experience firsthand the sensations and challenges faced by the riders, ensuring that his designs are not only safe but also exciting and functional.

For Nogué, feeling the wind on his face while testing a newly designed circuit is an indescribable experience that reflects his passion for motorsport and his commitment to excellence in track design.

His practical and detailed approach ensures that each circuit is a perfect combination of safety, performance, and excitement, benefiting both professional riders and enthusiasts.

30

In MotoGP, the margins of victory are often extremely narrow, reflecting the high level of competition and skill of the riders.

A notable example of this characteristic is the 2016 Italian Grand Prix, which has become a historic milestone in the world of MotoGP due to the incredibly close finish times between the riders.

During this Grand Prix, only 0.087 seconds separated the top two riders at the finish line when combining the results of the three categories: MotoGP, Moto2, and Moto3.

This fact underscores how competitive the races can be and how every millisecond counts in the fight for victory.

The Sunday at the 2016 Italian GP began with the Moto3 race, which turned out to be one of the most exciting and close-fought in history.

In this race, five riders crossed the finish line with a difference of just 0.077 seconds between them.

The final lap of the race was especially intense, with constant position changes and overtakes that kept spectators on the edge of their seats.

These narrow margins are the result of several factors, including the level of technology and development of the bikes, the skill and bravery of the riders, and the precision of team strategies.

In Moto3, in particular, where the bikes have limited power and the races are often tighter, it is common to see large groups of riders battling side by side until the very last moment.

31

MotoGP machines are true engineering marvels, designed to achieve impressive levels of performance and speed.

The roar of MotoGP engines can reach up to 128 decibels, which is extremely loud.

To put this in perspective, a pneumatic hammer produces a noise of approximately 104 decibels, making the sound of a MotoGP bike significantly louder and more powerful.

The brake discs on a MotoGP bike can reach temperatures of up to 750 °C.

These discs are designed to withstand the extreme conditions of intense and repetitive braking during a race.

The high temperature is indicative of the kinetic energy being dissipated as heat, which is crucial to ensure efficient and safe braking.

The materials used in these discs are advanced and designed to maintain their structural integrity at such high temperatures.

The grill of a MotoGP bike, referring to the areas around the engine and exhaust systems, can reach temperatures of around 250 °C.

This heat is generated by the engine and exhaust system and is a normal part of the operation of a high-performance bike.

Heat management is a critical aspect of the design of these bikes, as high temperatures can affect the performance and reliability of mechanical components.

In terms of engine speed, MotoGP bikes can reach up to 19,000 revolutions per minute (rpm).

This speed is extremely high compared to most common engines.

For example, a typical washing machine has an average spin speed of only 1,000 rpm.

The high engine speed in MotoGP bikes is essential to generate the power needed to reach the speeds seen in races, which can exceed 350 km/h on straightaways.

These facts highlight the extreme nature and technological sophistication of MotoGP bikes.

Every component, from the engine to the brakes and heat management, is designed to maximize performance under the most demanding conditions.

The high temperatures and extreme speeds at which these bikes operate require cutting-edge materials and technologies, as well as meticulous maintenance to ensure safety and performance in every race.

32

The most demanding corner for the braking system at the Lusail International Circuit is the first corner, due to the preceding long straight of 1,068 meters.

This straight allows MotoGP bikes to reach very high speeds before having to brake sharply to take the corner.

At this critical point on the circuit, the bikes must decelerate from 346 km/h to 99 km/h in just 5.3 seconds, covering a distance of 294 meters during this deceleration.

This process requires extreme precision and a tremendous capacity of the brakes to dissipate kinetic energy efficiently and safely.

To achieve such intense deceleration, riders apply a load of 5.2 kg on the brake lever.

This effort translates into a brake fluid pressure in the Brembo system that reaches 11.2 bar.

This high pressure is necessary to generate the braking force required to reduce speed in such a short time and space.

The braking systems of MotoGP bikes are designed to handle these extreme conditions.

The brake discs, typically made of carbon, offer excellent heat resistance and consistent braking performance even at the very high temperatures generated during intense braking.

Additionally, the brake calipers and pad materials are optimized to maximize friction and durability.

The first corner of the Lusail International Circuit tests not only the brakes but also the skill and precision of the riders, who must manage the deceleration to maintain control of the bike and position themselves correctly for the turn.

The performance of the brakes in this section of the circuit is crucial for safety and success in the race.

33

The revolution of wings in MotoGP had a crucial moment at the 2015 Qatar Grand Prix when Ducati unveiled the Desmosedici GP15.

This motorcycle represented a significant change in Ducati's strategy and design, notably differentiating itself from its predecessors in several key aspects.

In terms of the engine, the GP15 introduced improvements that optimized performance and efficiency, but one of the most notable innovations was the introduction of wing profiles in its design.

These aerodynamic profiles, or wings, were designed to increase the aerodynamic downforce on the bike, improving stability and handling, especially at high speeds and in corners.

The additional downforce helps keep the front wheel planted on the ground, reducing the risk of unintended wheelies and improving traction.

The Desmosedici GP15 is considered a cornerstone in Ducati's current dominance in MotoGP.

The adoption of these technologies and the focus on aerodynamics have allowed Ducati to develop faster and more manageable bikes, setting a new standard in the championship.

The GP15 marked the beginning of a new era for Ducati, in which they have continued to evolve and refine their aerodynamic approach.

In the same year, Brembo, a key supplier of braking systems in MotoGP, introduced high-strength aluminum brake calipers, specifically designed for use with high-mass brake pads.

These improved calipers offered greater rigidity and heat resistance, which is crucial under the extreme braking conditions experienced in MotoGP races.

The combination of these calipers with the high-mass brake pads provided superior braking performance, allowing riders to brake with greater precision and control.

The integration of these advancements in both the aerodynamic design of the bikes and the braking systems has allowed Ducati not only to improve on-track performance but also to set a trend that other teams have followed.

The introduction of wings and the improvements in brakes have changed the dynamics of MotoGP racing, making technology and engineering play an even more crucial role in achieving success in the championship.

34

The concept of "thumb power" in MotoGP dates back to 1992, when Australian rider Mick Doohan suffered a severe accident during qualifying at the Assen circuit.

Doohan crashed violently and was trapped underneath his Honda 500, almost costing him the amputation of his right leg.

The situation was critical, but Dr. Claudio Costa, founder of the Mobile Clinic, intervened to save not only Doohan's leg but also his career.

Dr. Costa made the decision to unofficially discharge Doohan from the hospital and transferred him to Italy.

There, Costa implemented an innovative and risky procedure: he sutured Doohan's two legs together for two weeks, allowing blood to flow from the healthy leg to the injured leg, which was in grave danger of failing.

This treatment was crucial for Doohan's recovery and allowed him to continue his career in MotoGP.

However, despite his recovery, Doohan still faced significant difficulties in modulating the force with his right leg, which affected his ability to effectively operate the rear brake.

It was then that Brembo engineers developed an innovative solution: the thumb-operated brake lever.

This device allowed Doohan to activate the rear brake using his left thumb instead of the traditional pedal.

This adaptation was key to enabling Doohan to compete at the highest level again and win races.

After its initial introduction and success, the thumb brake lever fell out of use for a couple of decades. However, in recent years, it has experienced a resurgence in MotoGP.

Many contemporary riders have adopted this technology to improve their control of the rear brake, especially in right-hand turns, where using the rear brake pedal effectively can be more challenging.

Using the thumb to operate the rear brake allows for greater precision and control, helping riders maintain stability and traction in critical situations.

35

The most difficult corner for the braking system at the Assen TT circuit is the first one after the finish line.

This corner presents a significant challenge due to the high speed at which MotoGP bikes arrive before having to brake sharply.

The bikes decelerate from 292 km/h to 106 km/h in just 4 seconds, covering a distance of 208 meters during this deceleration.

To achieve this rapid reduction in speed, riders apply a load of 5.4 kg on the brake lever.

This considerable effort translates into enormous braking force, generating a deceleration of 1.5 g.

The Brembo brake fluid pressure reaches 11.5 bar, indicating the high demand placed on the braking system during this process.

The intensive use of the brakes in this corner causes the temperature of the carbon brake discs to rise to 780 °C.

Carbon discs are preferred in MotoGP due to their ability to handle these high temperatures without losing effectiveness, unlike steel discs which can experience brake fade under similar conditions.

The combination of high speed, strong deceleration, and extreme temperatures tests both the riders' skill and the engineering of the bikes.

The ability of the brakes to maintain their performance under these conditions is crucial for safety and success in the race.

Additionally, temperature management is vital, as the brake discs and other components must dissipate heat quickly to avoid mechanical problems and maintain consistent braking.

The corner after the finish line at the Assen TT circuit is a perfect example of the complexity and demands of braking in MotoGP.

It requires a combination of precision, strength, and endurance from both the rider and the braking system.

The advanced design of Brembo brakes, along with the use of materials like carbon, allows riders to handle these extreme situations with confidence.

36

To date, the Motorcycle World Championship has seen 117 different riders crowned world champions across the various categories of the sport.

Giacomo Agostini holds the absolute record with an impressive total of 13 world titles, making him the most successful rider in the history of MotoGP and its predecessors.

Giacomo Agostini, affectionately known as "Ago," dominated the 1960s and 1970s, competing primarily for MV Agusta and later for Yamaha.

His titles are distributed between the 500cc (now MotoGP) and 350cc categories, with eight titles in 500cc and five in 350cc.

Following Agostini on the list of the most decorated riders are three riders with nine titles each: Mike Hailwood, Valentino Rossi, and Carlo Ubbiali.

Mike Hailwood, nicknamed "Mike the Bike," is remembered as one of the most versatile and talented riders in the history of motorcycling.

His nine world titles are spread across the 500cc, 350cc, and 250cc categories.

Hailwood is especially known for his ability to compete and win in multiple categories in the same season.

Valentino Rossi, known as "The Doctor," is one of the most iconic and popular riders of the modern MotoGP era.

His nine world titles include seven in the MotoGP (500cc) category and two in the 250cc and 125cc categories.

Rossi has been a key figure in motorcycling since the late 1990s and has greatly contributed to the global popularity of the sport.

Carlo Ubbiali, an Italian rider who excelled in the 1950s and 1960s, also has nine world titles.

He competed in the 125cc and 250cc categories and is remembered for his precision and consistency on the tracks.

Ubbiali was a pioneer in motorcycling and one of the first to reach such a number of titles.

These riders have not only amassed titles but also left an indelible mark on the history of motorcycling, each contributing to the development and popularity of the sport in their respective eras.

Their achievements are a testament to their skill, determination, and passion for racing, and they continue to inspire new generations of riders.

37

Throughout the history of the Motorcycle World Championship, a total of 718 riders have finished on the podium, meaning they placed in the top three across all categories.

This statistic reflects the wide diversity and talent that has passed through the different classes of the championship over the years.

Valentino Rossi is the rider who has stood on the podium the most, with a total of 234 occasions.

Rossi, known as "The Doctor," has had a long and successful career, excelling in the premier MotoGP category and being one of the most popular and charismatic riders in the history of the sport.

His ability to remain competitive for decades is a testament to his exceptional skill and dedication.

Giacomo Agostini, known as "Ago," ranks second on the list with 159 podiums.

Agostini, who competed primarily in the 1960s and 1970s, is a legend in motorcycling and remains the rider with the most world titles, with a total of 13.

His podiums are distributed across the 500cc (now MotoGP) and 350cc categories.

Dani Pedrosa, one of the most successful and consistent riders of the modern era, has stood on the podium 153 times.

Pedrosa, who competed for the Repsol Honda team, is known for his smooth riding style and his ability to compete at the highest level despite his small physical stature.

Throughout his career, he has been a constant contender in the MotoGP category.

Jorge Lorenzo, another standout rider from the Repsol Honda team, has 152 podiums to his name.

Lorenzo, a multiple world champion, is known for his precision and aggressiveness on the track.

His rivalry with Valentino Rossi and his success in the MotoGP category have been a significant part of his legacy in motorcycling.

Ángel Nieto, a legend in Spanish motorcycling, completes the top five with 139 podiums.

Nieto is one of the most successful riders in the lighter categories, with multiple titles in 50cc and 125cc.

His ability to dominate these classes made him an icon of the sport and a pivotal figure in the history of Spanish motorcycling.

38

The origin of the names of corners in MotoGP circuits is rich with history and tribute.

Many of these corners are named to honor legendary riders or commemorate significant moments in the sport of motorcycling.

This act of naming the corners is a way to preserve the memory of the figures and events that have left an indelible mark on MotoGP.

A prominent example is the "Doohan" corner at the Phillip Island circuit in Australia.

This corner is named after Mick Doohan, an Australian rider who won five world championships in the 500cc category, the direct predecessor of MotoGP.

Doohan is considered one of the greats in motorcycling, and naming a corner in his honor is a way to recognize his contribution and success in the sport.

In addition to honoring individual riders, some corners are named to reflect historical moments or specific characteristics of the circuit.

For example, at the Mugello circuit, the famous "Arrabbiata" corner (which means "angry" in Italian) is named for its challenging and fast nature, which tests the skill and courage of the riders.

In other cases, corners may bear local names or cultural references.

At the Jerez circuit in Spain, there is a corner named "Dry Sack," after a famous brand of Jerez wine, reflecting the rich winemaking tradition of the region.

These designations not only serve as a tribute but also add a distinctive and unique character to each circuit, giving each track its own identity and lore.

The names of the corners become part of the common language of fans and riders and help build an emotional and historical connection with the sport.

Naming corners in honor of legendary riders also inspires new generations of riders, who dream of leaving their own mark on the sport and perhaps one day having a corner named after them.

It is a constant reminder of past achievements and a motivation for future feats in the world of motorcycling.

39

The 2015 Japanese Grand Prix is remembered as one of the most controversial events in recent MotoGP history due to Valentino Rossi's accusations against Marc Márquez.

During this race, Rossi suggested that Márquez was deliberately helping Jorge Lorenzo win the world championship by interfering in his races.

Rossi accused Márquez of not competing with the intention of winning the race but rather of influencing the championship outcome in favor of Lorenzo, who was his compatriot and direct competitor for the title.

Rossi alleged that Márquez was playing tactically to hinder his progress and allow Lorenzo to accumulate more points.

According to Rossi, Márquez, who no longer had a chance to win the championship, was intentionally interfering to negatively affect his performance in the races.

These accusations intensified after it was observed that Márquez seemed to be fighting aggressively against Rossi while Lorenzo ran with little opposition.

The situation reached a boiling point during the 2015 Malaysian Grand Prix, which took place shortly after the initial accusations in Japan.

In Malaysia, Rossi and Márquez became involved in an on-track altercation that culminated in a controversial incident.

During the race, Rossi and Márquez were observed to have multiple position exchanges, culminating in a maneuver where Rossi appeared to force Márquez to the outside of the track, resulting in Márquez's fall.

The incident in Malaysia was investigated by the race stewards, who decided to penalize Rossi.

The penalty consisted of imposing three penalty points on his license and requiring him to start the last race of the season in Valencia from the back of the grid.

This sanction was highly debated and divided fans and analysts of motorcycling, as some supported the decision while others believed it was too severe or unjustified.

Despite Rossi's accusations, no conclusive evidence was ever found to prove that Márquez was deliberately helping Lorenzo.

Both riders and their respective teams denied any wrongdoing.

Lorenzo ultimately won the 2015 world championship, but the controversy surrounding Rossi's accusations and the incident in Malaysia cast a shadow over the season, and the relationships between Rossi, Márquez, and Lorenzo were seriously damaged.

40

The 2015 Valencia Grand Prix is another of the most controversial moments in MotoGP history, particularly due to the circumstances surrounding the championship battle between Valentino Rossi and Jorge Lorenzo.

This event was the final race of a season filled with tensions and controversies.

Valentino Rossi and Jorge Lorenzo arrived in Valencia as the main contenders for the world title; however, Rossi faced a significant disadvantage, having been penalized with the requirement to start the race from the last position on the grid due to an earlier incident with Marc Márquez at the Malaysian Grand Prix.

This incident had culminated in a penalty imposed on Rossi for a controversial maneuver that led to Márquez's crash.

The race in Valencia took place in an atmosphere of high tension.

Lorenzo started from pole position, while Rossi began from the last position.

During the race, Lorenzo maintained the lead, closely followed by Marc Márquez and Dani Pedrosa, both riders from Repsol Honda.

What generated controversy was the perception that Márquez and Pedrosa did not make serious attempts to overtake Lorenzo, despite seemingly having the pace to do so at certain points during the race.

This behavior fueled theories that Márquez was deliberately protecting Lorenzo's position to ensure he won the race and, consequently, the world championship.

Rossi and many of his supporters interpreted this lack of overtaking attempts as evidence of foul play, suggesting that Márquez was intentionally helping Lorenzo as a form of retaliation against Rossi for his previous accusations and the incident in Malaysia.

Rossi was particularly vocal in his criticism, claiming that Márquez acted as a "bodyguard" for Lorenzo during the race.

Despite the accusations and controversy, no concrete evidence was found that any rules had been broken.

Lorenzo won the race and, with it, secured his fifth world title and third in the MotoGP category.

MotoGP authorities and the International Motorcycling Federation (FIM) did not take any further disciplinary action against Márquez or Pedrosa, and Lorenzo was declared the legitimate world champion.

41

The 2008 United States Grand Prix at Laguna Seca is remembered for one of the most iconic duels in MotoGP history between Casey Stoner and Valentino Rossi.

This showdown was particularly highlighted by a daring and controversial overtaking maneuver by Rossi at the famous "Corkscrew" turn.

Laguna Seca is known for its difficult and technical "Corkscrew" turn, a downhill chicane with an abrupt change in direction and elevation, making it one of the most challenging corners on the MotoGP calendar.

During the 2008 race, Rossi and Stoner, who were in a fierce battle for the championship, engaged in an intense duel.

The most memorable moment of the race occurred when Rossi made a bold overtaking move on Stoner at the "Corkscrew."

In a daring maneuver, Rossi partially went off the track, passing through the gravel before returning to the asphalt just ahead of Stoner.

This overtaking move was considered by many to be extremely risky and bordering on the edge of the rules.

Stoner, who was racing with Ducati at the time, complained about Rossi's maneuver, calling it too aggressive and even dangerous.

However, the race authorities did not impose any penalty on Rossi, considering that the overtaking, while risky, was within the acceptable limits of competition.

The incident generated great controversy and division of opinions among MotoGP fans and analysts.

Some applauded Rossi's maneuver as a display of his bravery and exceptional skill, while others criticized the lack of a penalty and considered the move unsporting.

Despite Stoner's complaints, Rossi retained his victory in the race, and this moment became one of the most iconic of his career.

The 2008 race at Laguna Seca is frequently remembered and mentioned in debates about the most memorable and controversial overtakes in MotoGP history.

The duel between Rossi and Stoner at Laguna Seca also highlighted the different interpretations that can arise from on-track actions.

In motorsport, where decisions are made in split seconds and under intense pressure, maneuvers can be viewed in various ways, generating controversy and discussions about sportsmanship and the rules.

42

During the 2016 Malaysian Grand Prix at Sepang, new tensions arose between Jorge Lorenzo, Valentino Rossi, and Marc Márquez.

Lorenzo hinted that Rossi and Márquez were conspiring to influence the race results, suggesting that Márquez was deliberately blocking his progress to benefit Rossi.

Lorenzo claimed that Márquez, instead of competing for the win, was strategically acting to hinder his advancement and help Rossi secure a better position in the race and, consequently, in the championship.

These accusations were based on the perception that Márquez was actively intervening in the battle between Lorenzo and Rossi, which heightened the tension among the riders.

These insinuations could not be proven, and there was no concrete evidence to support Lorenzo's claims; however, the accusations alone were enough to exacerbate an already complicated relationship between the three riders.

The previous history of conflicts and rivalries between Rossi, Márquez, and Lorenzo contributed to these accusations being taken seriously by some and dismissed by others.

This incident at Sepang 2016 is part of a series of events that have marked the relationships between these riders.

As early as 2015, controversies and accusations of unsporting behavior had significantly strained the atmosphere in MotoGP.

Lorenzo's insinuations in 2016 reignited these tensions and added another layer of controversy to the championship.

The relationships between Rossi and Márquez, in particular, had been tense since the incident at Sepang in 2015, where Rossi accused Márquez of interfering in the championship battle in favor of Lorenzo.

This background made Lorenzo's new accusations in 2016 resonate even more in the context of the championship.

The situation also reflected how personal dynamics and rivalries can influence perceptions and accusations within the sport.

43

MotoGP Riders' Nutrition.

1. Breakfast:
- **Time:** Generally between 6:30 and 8:00 AM.
- **Objective:** Provide sustained energy for the start of the day and morning training sessions.
- **Composition:**
  - **Complex Carbohydrates:** Oatmeal with fresh fruits such as banana, berries, or apple, and a bit of honey for quick energy.
  - **Proteins:** Scrambled or boiled eggs, sometimes accompanied by spinach and avocado.
  - **Healthy Fats:** Avocado, nuts, or seeds like chia or flaxseed.
  - **Beverages:** Water, green tea, or coffee (in moderation). A protein shake with plant-based milk and fruits is also common.

2. Morning Snack:
- **Time:** Between 10:00 and 11:00 AM.
- **Objective:** Maintain energy levels and stave off hunger before lunch.
- **Composition:**
  - **Fresh Fruits:** Apple, banana, or berries.
  - **Light Proteins:** Natural Greek yogurt or a small portion of nuts.
  - **Hydration:** Water or isotonic drinks to replenish electrolytes.

3. Lunch:
- **Time:** Generally between 12:30 and 2:00 PM.
- **Objective:** Provide energy for afternoon training or track activities.
- **Composition:**
  - **Lean Proteins:** Grilled chicken, fish such as salmon or tuna, or tofu for vegetarian options.
  - **Complex Carbohydrates:** Quinoa, brown rice, whole wheat pasta, or sweet potato.
  - **Vegetables:** Green salad with spinach, arugula, carrots, cucumbers, and bell peppers. Light dressing with olive oil and lemon.

- **Healthy Fats:** Olive oil, avocado, or a small portion of nuts.
- **Hydration:** Water or an isotonic drink.

4. Afternoon Snack:
- **Time:** Between 3:30 and 5:00 PM.
- **Objective:** Maintain energy levels for afternoon training or recovery activities.
- **Composition:**
  - **Proteins:** A protein shake, a handful of almonds, or a low-sugar protein bar.
  - **Carbohydrates:** A piece of fruit or a small portion of granola.
  - **Hydration:** Water or a low-calorie sports drink.

5. Dinner:
- **Time:** Generally between 7:00 and 8:30 PM.
- **Objective:** Muscle recovery and energy replenishment after a day of training or competition.
- **Composition:**
  - **Lean Proteins:** Fatty fish like salmon or trout, chicken, turkey, or a vegetarian option like tofu or legumes.
  - **Complex Carbohydrates:** Brown rice, quinoa, or whole wheat pasta.
  - **Vegetables:** Steamed or roasted vegetables like broccoli, kale, carrots, and zucchini.
  - **Healthy Fats:** Olive oil for cooking or dressing, avocado, or a portion of nuts.
  - **Hydration:** Water and occasionally an infusion or caffeine-free tea.

6. Night Snack (if needed):
- **Time:** Between 9:00 and 10:00 PM.
- **Objective:** Ensure proper muscle recovery and prevent nighttime hunger.
- **Composition:**
  - **Proteins:** A small protein shake, Greek yogurt, or a glass of almond milk.
  - **Hydration:** Water.

7. Additional Considerations:
Supplements such as protein powders, amino acids, multivitamins, and specific minerals like magnesium and zinc are commonly used to ensure adequate intake of essential nutrients.

44

Marc Márquez is known for his highly aggressive riding style, characterized by extremely steep lean angles in the corners.

While most MotoGP riders typically lean their bikes up to about 60 degrees relative to the pavement, Márquez has managed to exceed even 68 degrees of lean without falling.

This ability to lean the bike at such extreme angles allows him to maintain higher speeds through corners and improve his lap times.

To achieve and maintain these lean angles, Márquez uses a combination of advanced techniques and exceptional bike control.

These include:

- **Weight Distribution:** Márquez shifts his weight optimally on the bike, moving his body towards the inside of the corner to lower the center of gravity and increase traction.
- **Body Use:** His style includes precise and controlled body movements, using his knees and elbows to stabilize the bike. It's common to see Márquez dragging his elbow on the ground in the tightest corners.
- **Bike Setup:** Márquez's bike, prepared by the Repsol Honda team, is specifically tuned to allow him to make the most of his riding style. This includes customized settings for the suspension, chassis, and tires.

Márquez's riding style is not without risks.

The extreme lean angles increase the probability of crashes if traction is lost, if there are irregularities on the track, or if a mistake is made.

However, Márquez's ability to regain control in seemingly lost situations is remarkable.

There have been numerous occasions where he has avoided imminent crashes thanks to his agility and reflexes.

To maintain this level of control and performance, Márquez follows a rigorous physical and mental training regimen.

His preparation includes:

- **Muscle Strengthening:** Specific exercises to strengthen core muscles and limbs, essential for control and stability on the bike.
- **Endurance Training:** Cardiovascular activities like running, cycling, and swimming to improve endurance and aerobic capacity.
- **Flexibility and Mobility:** Stretching and yoga programs to maintain flexibility, crucial for extreme movements on the bike.
- **Mental Training:** Visualization and concentration techniques to improve quick decision-making and response to high-pressure situations.

Márquez's style has influenced other riders and the development of MotoGP bikes.

His success and ability to push the bike to its limits have led teams and riders to reevaluate and adapt their own techniques and setups to stay competitive.

45

The Most Expensive and Sophisticated Helmets in MotoGP.

1. Arai Corsair-X RC (Racing Carbon)
- **Price:** Approximately $4,000 USD
- **Details:** This helmet from Arai is one of the most expensive available in the MotoGP market. It is constructed with an aviation-grade carbon fiber shell, making it extremely lightweight and strong. The aerodynamic design includes an advanced ventilation system and a fully removable and washable interior. Arai is known for its meticulous attention to detail and commitment to safety.

2. AGV Pista GP RR
- **Price:** Approximately $1,400 - $1,600 USD
- **Details:** Used by elite riders like Valentino Rossi, the AGV Pista GP RR is known for its aerodynamic design and advanced technology. It is made of a blend of carbon fiber and Kevlar, providing excellent protection and lightness. The helmet features an optimized ventilation system and a customizable interior for a perfect fit.

3. Shoei X-Fourteen
- **Price:** Approximately $800 - $900 USD
- **Details:** The Shoei X-Fourteen is popular among many MotoGP riders. It is made with an AIM+ (Advanced Integrated Matrix Plus Multi-Fiber) shell that provides high strength and great impact absorption. The design includes an effective ventilation system and a fully removable and washable interior. Shoei also offers customization to fit the specific preferences of riders.

4. HJC RPHA 11 Pro
- **Price:** Approximately $600 - $700 USD
- **Details:** Used by riders like Cal Crutchlow, the HJC RPHA 11 Pro is designed for high-performance racing. The shell is made of PIM+ (Premium Integrated Matrix Plus), which combines various materials like carbon fiber and aramid to offer excellent protection and lightness. The helmet also includes an advanced ventilation system and a comfortable, adjustable interior.

5. Nolan X-803 Ultra Carbon.

- **Price:** Approximately $700 - $800 USD
- **Details:** This Nolan helmet is made of ultra-light carbon fiber, making it very light and strong. It features an advanced ventilation system and a comfortable, customizable interior. Nolan is known for its high standards of safety and comfort, making it a popular choice among professional and amateur riders.

Common Features and Technologies in Helmets:

1. High-tech materials: The most expensive helmets are made from advanced materials like carbon fiber, Kevlar, and aramid, providing high impact resistance and being extremely lightweight.

2. Aerodynamic design: Helmets are designed to minimize wind resistance and improve stability at high speeds. This includes aerodynamic shapes and integrated spoilers.

3. Advanced ventilation system: Ventilation is crucial to keep the rider's head cool and comfortable during races. High-end helmets have multiple air inlets and outlets for optimal ventilation.

4. Customizable interior: The interior of the helmets can be fully removable and washable, and is often customizable to ensure a perfect fit. This includes different-sized pads and fine-tuning adjustment systems.

5. High-quality visor systems: Visors are usually high-quality, with anti-fog and scratch-resistant treatments. Some models also include photochromic visors or quick-release systems for easy visor changes.

6. Safety and certifications: All helmets used in MotoGP must meet strict safety regulations, such as ECE, DOT, and Snell certification. This ensures that the helmets provide maximum protection in case of an accident.

46

The most expensive MotoGP bike is a highly sophisticated machine that represents the pinnacle of technology and engineering in motorcycling.

These bikes are designed to be extremely fast, light, and safe, with every component optimized for maximum performance.

1. General Cost of a MotoGP Bike: It can vary depending on several factors, including specific components, technology used, and continuous development throughout the season. However, it is estimated that the price of a MotoGP bike can range between 2 and 3 million dollars (USD).

2. Cost Breakdown:
- **Engine:** The engine is one of the most expensive parts of the bike, with a cost that can reach 250,000 to 300,000 USD. These engines are highly advanced, with specifications including multiple cylinders, high displacement, and components made of lightweight and durable materials such as titanium and carbon fiber.
- **Chassis and Structure:** The chassis, generally made of carbon fiber composites or lightweight alloys, can cost around 100,000 USD. The design of the chassis is crucial for the bike's maneuverability and stability.
- **Electronics and Telemetry:** The electronic system, which includes the engine control unit (ECU), sensors, and telemetry systems, can cost between 100,000 and 150,000 USD. These systems allow for precise and real-time adjustments of the bike's parameters, as well as the collection of vital performance data for analysis.
- **Suspension and Brakes:** Advanced suspension from manufacturers like Ohlins and high-tech braking systems from brands like Brembo can cost between 50,000 and 80,000 USD. These components are essential for the bike's control and safety at high speeds.

- Tires: The special MotoGP tires, primarily supplied by Michelin, have a significant cost and are designed to provide maximum grip and durability under racing conditions.
Each set of tires can cost around 1,500 USD, and teams use multiple sets during a race weekend.

- Aerodynamics: Fairings and other aerodynamic components made of carbon fiber can cost tens of thousands of dollars. Aerodynamics are crucial for the bike's top speed and stability on the track.

3. Continuous Development: The cost of a MotoGP bike is not fixed, as teams continuously invest in the development and improvement of their machines throughout the season. This includes researching and developing new components, implementing improvements based on race data, and maintaining the bike.

4. Teams and Personnel: In addition to the cost of the bike itself, MotoGP teams also incur significant expenses to pay for technical and support personnel, including engineers, mechanics, data analysts, and other specialists.
This personnel is essential for maintaining and optimizing the bike's performance throughout the season.

5. Comparison with Production Bikes: To put these costs into perspective, the most expensive production bikes on the market, such as the Ducati Panigale V4 R or the Honda RC213V-S (a street version of Honda's MotoGP bike), are priced between 100,000 and 200,000 USD.
These production bikes are significantly less expensive than the actual MotoGP machines due to differences in technology, materials, and development.

47

In the history of the Motorcycle World Championship, 372 different riders have had the honor of standing on the top step of the podium.

This reflects the diversity and talent that has passed through the various categories of the sport over the years.

Below are some key aspects and statistics about these riders and their victories:

Leaders in Number of Wins:

1. Giacomo Agostini:
- **Wins:** 122
- **Details:** Giacomo Agostini is the rider with the most wins in the history of the Motorcycle World Championship. He competed primarily in the 1960s and 1970s, achieving most of his victories in the 500cc and 350cc categories. His dominance with MV Agusta and later with Yamaha has secured him a prominent place in the sport's history.

2. Valentino Rossi:
- **Wins:** 115
- **Details:** Valentino Rossi, known as "The Doctor," is one of the most iconic and popular riders in nmotorcycling. Competing mainly in the MotoGP category (formerly 500cc), Rossi has won titles and races with Honda and Yamaha. His riding style and charisma have left an indelible mark on the sport.

3. Ángel Nieto:

- **Wins:** 90
- **Details:** Ángel Nieto, a legend of Spanish motorcycling, won his victories primarily in the 50cc and 125cc categories. Nieto is remembered for his skill and prowess in the lighter categories, and his legacy endures in Spanish motorcycling.

4. Mike Hailwood:

- **Wins:** 76
- **Details:** Mike Hailwood, known as "Mike the Bike," is famous for his versatility and success in multiple categories. He competed in 500cc, 350cc, and 250cc, standing out for his ability to adapt to different bikes and conditions.

5. Marc Márquez:

- **Wins:** 73
- **Details:** Marc Márquez, a rider for the Repsol Honda team, has achieved his victories in the MotoGP category. Known for his aggressive style and ability to push the limits, Márquez has been one of the most dominant riders of the modern era.

Riders with a Single Victory:

Of the 372 winners, 111 have managed to stand on the top step of the podium in a Grand Prix only once.

These riders have experienced success on one occasion, highlighting how difficult and competitive it is to win in the Motorcycle World Championship.

Some riders who have managed to stand on the top step of the podium only once in their career:

- **Danilo Petrucci** - Italy, Mugello 2019 (Ducati)
- **Chris Vermeulen** - Australia, Le Mans 2007 (Suzuki)
- **Troy Bayliss** - Australia, Valencia 2006 (Ducati)
- **Karel Abraham** - Czech Republic, Valencia 2010 (Moto2, Ducati)
- **Mika Kallio -** Finland, Donington Park 2009 (Moto2, KTM)
- **Sete Gibernau** - Spain, Valencia 2001 (Suzuki)
- **John Kocinski** - United States, Australia 1993 (Cagiva)
- **Régis Laconi** - France, Valencia 1999 (Yamaha)
- **Alex Barros** - Brazil, Imola 2000 (Honda)
  (It took him 10 years to achieve his only victory)
- **Tetsuya Harada** - Japan, Brno 2001 (Aprilia)
- **Ben Spies** - United States, Assen 2011 (Yamaha)
- **Jack Middelburg** - Netherlands, Silverstone 1981 (Suzuki)
- **Andrea Iannone** - Italy, Red Bull Ring 2016 (Ducati)
- **Noboru Ueda** - Japan, Suzuka 1991 (125cc, Honda)

48

The Motorcycle World Championship has seen riders from 29 different nationalities stand on the top step of the podium throughout its history, demonstrating the diversity and global nature of the sport.

Italy is the most successful country in the history of motorcycling, leading the rankings with 811 victories.

This success is largely due to legendary riders such as Giacomo Agostini, Valentino Rossi, and Carlo Ubbiali, who have dominated multiple categories and eras.

Italy also has a rich history of motorcycle manufacturers, such as Ducati, Aprilia, and MV Agusta, which have contributed to the success of Italian riders.

Spain ranks second with 609 victories.

In recent decades, riders like Ángel Nieto, Jorge Lorenzo, Marc Márquez, and Dani Pedrosa have been crucial to Spain's success in motorcycling.

Spain has also produced many young talents who have dominated the lower categories before moving up to MotoGP.

The training structure and national competitions in Spain are very strong, which has helped nurture many champions.

Great Britain has a rich history in motorcycling, with 383 victories.

Riders like Mike Hailwood, Geoff Duke, and Barry Sheene are some of the most notable names.

Although the number of British riders in MotoGP has decreased in recent years, their historical legacy in the sport is significant.

Germany has achieved 191 victories in the history of motorcycling.

Notable German riders include Anton Mang and Dieter Braun.

Germany's presence in the top categories has been less prominent in recent decades, but they remain a force to be reckoned with, especially in the lighter categories and European competitions.

Australia has produced some of the most iconic riders in motorcycling, amassing 180 victories.

Riders like Mick Doohan, Casey Stoner, and Wayne Gardner have left an indelible mark on the sport.

Australia's heritage in MotoGP is strong, and their riders have been known for their aggressive style and ability to dominate in different track conditions.

While Italy, Spain, Great Britain, Germany, and Australia lead the rankings, it is important to mention that other nationalities have also found success in MotoGP.

The United States has seen riders like Kenny Roberts, Eddie Lawson, and Kevin Schwantz contribute to a significant total of victories, particularly in the 1970s, 1980s, and 1990s.

France, with riders like Christian Sarron and more recently Fabio Quartararo, has seen a resurgence in motorcycling.

Japan, with riders such as Norick Abe and Daijiro Kato, remains a key country in the production of motorcycles and technology for the sport.

49

Since its inception, the Motorcycle World Championship has had a truly global reach, traveling to 30 different countries throughout its history.

This championship has been held at various circuits around the world, reflecting the popularity and importance of motorcycling in diverse cultures and regions.

Spain is the country that has hosted the most races in the history of the Motorcycle World Championship, with 400 races.

With a rich tradition in motorcycling and a fervent passion for the sport, Spain has hosted numerous races at iconic circuits.

Some of the most well-known circuits in Spain include the Circuito de Jerez, the Circuit de Barcelona-Catalunya, the Circuit Ricardo Tormo in Valencia, and the MotorLand Aragón.

These events have been fundamental to the development of motorcycling in Spain and have contributed to the training of many Spanish world champions.

Italy ranks second with 347 races hosted.

Italy has a deeply rooted history in motorcycling, both in terms of riders and motorcycle manufacturers.

Legendary circuits such as Mugello and Misano have witnessed numerous epic battles and are considered temples of motorcycling.

The Italian passion for motorcycles is evident at every event, with large crowds and a vibrant atmosphere.

The United Kingdom has been a pillar of motorcycling since its beginnings, with historic circuits and a very passionate fan base.

Silverstone, in particular, is known for its fast layout and its importance on the MotoGP calendar.

Germany has hosted numerous races over the years, featuring technical and challenging circuits.

Sachsenring is one of the most well-known, famous for its technical layout and unique atmosphere.

Japan is a key country in motorcycling, not only for its riders but also for its motorcycle manufacturers such as Honda, Yamaha, and Suzuki.

Twin Ring Motegi is a modern circuit that combines technical and fast sections.

The United States has had a significant presence in MotoGP, with iconic circuits like Laguna Seca, known for its famous "Corkscrew" turn.

The Circuit of the Americas in Texas is one of the most modern circuits on the calendar.

Phillip Island in Australia is one of the most beloved and spectacular circuits in the MotoGP calendar.

Its coastal location and fast, flowing design make it a favorite for both riders and fans.

Assen in the Netherlands, known as the "Cathedral" of motorcycling, has been an emblematic venue for the championship.

It is one of the oldest and most revered circuits, with a design that has evolved over the years to maintain its relevance and challenge.

France has hosted numerous races, with Le Mans being one of the most recognized circuits.

The history and tradition of motorcycling in France are reflected in the popularity of these events.

50

Honda remains the most successful manufacturer in the history of the Motorcycle World Championship, amassing a total of 776 victories across all categories.

This achievement highlights Honda's consistency and technical excellence over the years.

Founded in 1948, Honda has been at the forefront of developing racing motorcycles, and its success is due to a combination of technological innovation, rider talent, and a strong racing program.

Yamaha ranks second with 502 victories.

Yamaha, another giant in the world of motorcycling, has been a fierce competitor since its entry into motorcycle racing.

Its success is partly due to close collaboration with renowned riders like Valentino Rossi, Jorge Lorenzo, and Kenny Roberts, who have significantly contributed to its record.

Aprilia has achieved 294 victories, positioning itself as one of the most successful manufacturers, especially in the smaller displacement categories like 125cc and 250cc.

Aprilia is known for its focus on innovation and the development of advanced technologies, which have resulted in highly competitive and successful bikes in the championship.

MV Agusta, with 275 victories, was an absolute dominant force during the 1950s and 1960s.

Legendary riders like Giacomo Agostini took MV Agusta to the top, cementing its legacy in the history of motorcycling.

Although their presence in the championship has diminished in recent decades, their historical impact remains significant.

Suzuki, with 157 victories, has also been a key competitor in the Motorcycle World Championship.

Suzuki has achieved great success thanks to riders like Barry Sheene, Kevin Schwantz, and more recently, Joan Mir, who won the MotoGP championship in 2020.

Suzuki's ability to produce fast and reliable bikes has been crucial to their victories.

51

Women in MotoGP have had a limited presence, but some have made a significant mark in the history of motorcycling.

Ana Carrasco is one of the most notable examples.

In 2018, Carrasco became the first woman to win a motorcycle racing world championship, achieving this milestone in the Supersport 300 category.

Her victory not only highlighted her talent and determination but also opened doors and served as an inspiration for other women in the sport.

In addition to Carrasco, other women have competed in various categories of the Motorcycle World Championship.

For example, Taru Rinne and Tomoko Igata competed in the 125cc category in the 1990s, while María Herrera has competed in the Moto3 and MotoE categories, demonstrating that women can compete at the highest level in motorcycling.

The path for women in MotoGP and motorcycling in general has been challenging, mainly due to the historically male-dominated nature of the sport.

Nonetheless, the growing visibility and success of riders like Carrasco and Herrera are changing perceptions and encouraging more women to pursue careers in this field.

The inclusion and success of women in MotoGP have also led to a greater focus on gender equality within the sport, with initiatives and programs designed to support and promote female participation.

These efforts include rider academies and development programs that seek to identify and nurture female talent from a young age.

52

Tires play a crucial role in MotoGP.

Michelin is the official tire supplier, and teams must carefully choose between different compounds (soft, medium, hard) depending on track conditions and weather.

Soft tires provide greater grip and allow for faster lap times but wear out more quickly.

Medium tires offer a balance between grip and durability, while hard tires are more durable but provide less grip.

Choosing the right tire is essential for race performance.

A wrong choice can result in premature wear, loss of grip, or even tire failure, which can cost valuable seconds each lap and ultimately the race.

Teams conduct a thorough analysis of track and weather conditions before each session to decide which compound to use.

Track temperature, asphalt abrasiveness, and weather conditions such as rain or sunshine play a crucial role in this decision.

During the race, riders must also manage tire wear and adjust their riding style to maximize tire life.

Additionally, practice and qualifying sessions are vital for testing different compounds and setups to find the best possible combination for the race.

Tire pressure is another critical factor, as it affects grip and the tire's operating temperature.

Teams work with real-time data and use telemetry to monitor and adjust tire pressure during sessions.

53

Recently, the "Holeshot Device" has gained popularity in MotoGP due to its ability to significantly improve riders' starts from the starting line.

This device, initially introduced by Ducati, modifies the geometry of the bike to reduce wheelies and improve initial traction.

A wheelie is a common phenomenon during quick starts, where the engine's power lifts the front wheel off the ground, which can reduce acceleration and make the bike harder to control.

The "Holeshot Device" works by locking the rear suspension in a compressed position, lowering the bike's center of gravity and increasing stability.

This allows the engine's power to transfer more efficiently to the ground, improving traction and enabling faster and more controlled acceleration.

By keeping the front wheel on the ground, riders can apply more power without worrying about losing control due to an unexpected wheelie.

The device is manually activated by the rider before the race start.

Once the bike begins to move and reaches a certain speed, the "Holeshot Device" deactivates automatically, allowing the rear suspension to return to its normal configuration for the rest of the race.

This quick and controlled change is crucial for maximizing performance during the early stages of the race, where a good start can make a significant difference in position and overall strategy.

The adoption of the "Holeshot Device" is not limited to Ducati; other manufacturers like Yamaha, Suzuki, Honda, and KTM have also developed and are using versions of this device on their race bikes.

The implementation and refinement of this technology have led to increased competitiveness at the start, making the first lap of races even more exciting and contested.

In addition to improving starts, the "Holeshot Device" can also be beneficial in other parts of the circuit, such as slow corners where acceleration out of the turn is crucial.

Some teams are exploring how to use the device in different situations during the race to gain additional advantages.

54

**Aerodynamics has taken on a crucial role
in the design of MotoGP bikes in recent years.**

Teams invest significantly in wind tunnels and simulations
to optimize the shape of the bikes, aiming to maximize
aerodynamic efficiency and improve on-track performance.

This approach includes the addition of wings and other
aerodynamic devices to enhance stability and speed,
especially in corners and at high speeds.

One of the most notable developments in MotoGP
aerodynamics has been the incorporation of
aerodynamic wings on the bikes.

These wings, initially introduced by Ducati, are designed
to generate downforce, pressing the bike down to improve
traction and stability.

Downforce helps keep the front wheel on the ground during
acceleration, reduces wheelies, and improves behavior
during braking and cornering.

The wings also contribute to lateral stability, allowing riders
to maintain higher speeds in corners without losing control.

Initially, aerodynamic wings were a subject of controversy.

Some riders and teams expressed concerns about safety
and the impact on bike behavior in racing situations.

However, over time, the aerodynamic advantages proved
to be significant, and most teams began to adopt and
develop their own aerodynamic solutions.

The International Motorcycling Federation (FIM) and Dorna Sports, organizers of MotoGP, have established specific regulations to control the design and use of these devices, ensuring a balance between innovation and safety.

The use of wind tunnels and computer simulations is fundamental in the aerodynamic development of the bikes.

In wind tunnels, full-scale bikes or scale models are tested to study how air flows around them.

This allows engineers to identify areas for improvement and adjust the design of fairings, wings, and other components to reduce air resistance and increase downforce where necessary.

Computer simulations complement these physical tests, allowing for quick and precise design iterations before building and testing physical components.

Aerodynamic optimization is not limited to the wings alone.

Teams also work on the shape of the fairing, the position of the exhaust, cooling ducts, and other elements that affect the airflow around the bike.

All of this contributes to more efficient and stable performance, improving top speed, acceleration, and maneuverability in various racing conditions.

55
The Longest Championship.

The 2020 MotoGP season was notably long due to the COVID-19 pandemic, with multiple rescheduling and adjustments.

The pandemic significantly impacted the original calendar, forcing organizers to cancel or postpone several races.

However, despite these challenges, the season was restructured to hold 14 races over a period of 18 weeks.

This adjustment required great coordination and flexibility from the teams, riders, and organizers, who worked tirelessly to adapt the championship to the changing circumstances.

The races took place at a variety of circuits, some of which were used more than once to make up for the cancellation of other events.

For example, the Circuito de Jerez in Spain hosted two consecutive Grands Prix at the start of the season, while the Red Bull Ring in Austria also hosted two consecutive races.

This approach not only helped reduce international travel and logistical complications but also allowed teams and riders to focus on their performance in a more controlled environment.

Throughout the season, strict safety protocols were implemented to protect the health of everyone involved.

These protocols included regular COVID-19 testing, social distancing measures, and restricted access to paddock areas.

Despite the difficulties, the 2020 season demonstrated the sport's adaptability and resilience.

Teams and riders had to face not only the usual competition challenges but also the additional uncertainties and tensions caused by the pandemic.

The 2020 championship was also notable for the intense competition and unpredictability of the results.

Several riders stood out throughout the season, and the championship battle remained open until the final races.

The ability of the teams to quickly adapt to the new conditions and maintain a high level of performance was crucial for the season's success.

56

The Sachsenring circuit in Germany is known for being the shortest on the MotoGP calendar, with a length of 3.7 km.

This circuit, located in the Saxony region, is famous for its technical and challenging design, which includes many tight corners and elevation changes.

The compact nature of Sachsenring makes it a challenge for riders, who must demonstrate precision and constant control.

Additionally, the short length of the circuit means that races are often very intense and competitive, with riders constantly in traffic and fighting for positions.

In contrast, the Silverstone Circuit in Great Britain is one of the longest on the MotoGP calendar, with a length of 5.9 km.

Silverstone, located in Northamptonshire, is a legendary circuit known for its high speed and long straights combined with a variety of fast and technical corners.

The length of the circuit allows riders to reach very high speeds, and the variety of corners presents a diverse challenge in terms of technique and strategy.

Silverstone has hosted numerous memorable MotoGP races, and its long track offers many opportunities for overtaking and complex race strategies.

The difference between these two circuits reflects the diversity of the MotoGP calendar, where riders must adapt to a wide range of conditions and track styles.

Mayweather has been nicknamed "Money" due to his ability to generate enormous sums of money both inside and outside the ring.

He is known for his business acumen and for being one of the highest-paid athletes in the world.

Throughout his career, he has amassed an estimated fortune of hundreds of millions of dollars, primarily through fight purses, pay-per-view deals, and sponsorship contracts.

In addition to his financial success, Mayweather is known for his extravagant lifestyle.

He frequently showcases his wealth on social media, displaying luxury cars, expensive jewelry, and impressive properties.

His company, Mayweather Promotions, has also played a crucial role in his ability to maximize his earnings, as he has had direct control over his fight contracts and promotions.

Outside the ring, Mayweather has had his share of controversies.

He has faced legal issues, including accusations of domestic violence, which have tarnished his reputation.

Nonetheless, his ability to remain undefeated and his business prowess have kept him in the spotlight.

57

Jorge Martín is a Spanish rider who has made history in MotoGP by setting a new top speed record.

During the Italian Grand Prix at the Mugello Circuit, Martín reached a speed of 363.6 km/h on his Ducati Desmosedici.

This impressive achievement not only highlights his skill and bravery as a rider but also the power and efficiency of the bike he rides.

The Ducati Desmosedici, known for being one of the fastest and most powerful bikes on the MotoGP grid, has been continuously optimized by the Ducati team to maximize its performance.

The combination of a highly advanced engine, refined aerodynamics, and sophisticated electronic management has allowed the Desmosedici to reach astounding speeds.

Jorge Martín, taking full advantage of these capabilities, surpassed the previous top speed record, underscoring the ongoing evolution and technological development in the sport.

Martín, born on January 29, 1998, in Madrid, Spain, began his career in lower categories of motorcycling, quickly standing out for his talent and determination.

His rise in MotoGP has been meteoric, and he has proven to be a fierce competitor and an extremely fast rider.

His top speed record at Mugello is a testament to his ability to push the limits and extract maximum performance from his bike.

The Italian Grand Prix at Mugello is known for its long main straight, where bikes can reach very high speeds.

This circuit is particularly suitable for top speed tests due to its design and the quality of its surface.

The combination of Martín's skills, the power of the Ducati, and the optimal conditions of the circuit allowed for this new record to be set.

The ability to reach such speeds in MotoGP depends not only on the rider and the bike but also on a series of technical and strategic factors.

The bike's setup, including aerodynamics, engine management, and tire choice, plays a crucial role.

Additionally, the rider's ability to handle the bike at extreme speeds while maintaining control and stability is essential for achieving and sustaining top speed records.

Jorge Martín's achievement has been widely recognized and celebrated in the world of motorcycling.

His record not only stands out in terms of statistics but also reflects the competitive spirit and constant innovation in MotoGP.

The pursuit of speed and performance remains an integral part of the sport, and riders like Martín continue to raise the bar and set new standards for future generations.

58

The first victory by a wildcard in the premier class of the Motorcycle World Championship occurred in 1998, when Japanese rider Norick Abe won the Japanese Grand Prix at Suzuka.

This victory was historic and memorable, especially for Japanese fans, as it marked a significant milestone in the sport.

Norick Abe, known for his aggressive riding style and natural talent, entered the Suzuka race as a wildcard, a position granted to riders who do not compete full-time in the series but have the opportunity to participate in certain races.

Abe was already a respected and well-known rider in motorcycling, having shown flashes of his potential in previous races, but his victory at Suzuka was unexpected and electrifying.

During the race, Abe displayed exceptional skill and determination.

He maximized his knowledge of the circuit and the advantage of racing in his home country.

The race at Suzuka was intense and competitive, but Abe managed to stay in the lead, handling the pressure impressively.

His victory was not only a great joy for him and his team but also a moment of pride for the Japanese fans who fervently supported him.

This wildcard victory was particularly significant because it showed that riders who are not full-time competitors in the championship can still compete at the highest level and win.

It was proof that talent and skill can overcome the disadvantages of not having a full season of experience and preparation.

Norick Abe's career continued after this historic victory, and although he did not win another Grand Prix, his triumph at Suzuka became a highlight of his career and a significant moment in the history of the Motorcycle World Championship.

Abe became a symbol of hope and motivation for other Japanese riders and young talents aspiring to achieve success in international motorcycling.

59

The 2017 Japanese Grand Prix at Motegi is known for having one of the highest numbers of overtakes in a single race, highlighting the fierce competition among the riders.

This race is especially remembered for the intense battle between Andrea Dovizioso and Marc Márquez, two of the strongest contenders of the season.

The weather conditions during the race were extremely challenging, with constant rain turning the circuit into a very tricky setting.

These conditions made bike control and the riders' ability to manage grip crucial, increasing the number of errors and opportunities for overtakes.

From the start of the race, it was clear that it would be an epic battle.

Marc Márquez, known for his aggression and ability to handle tricky situations, was in his element, but Andrea Dovizioso, with his calculated and precise riding style, was determined to challenge him to the end.

Throughout the race, both riders exchanged positions multiple times, creating an exciting spectacle for the spectators.

The competition was so tight that each lap seemed to have a new leader, with overtakes happening in almost every section of the circuit.

This rivalry led to one of the highest numbers of overtakes recorded in a MotoGP race, keeping the fans on the edge of their seats.

The tension reached its peak in the final laps.

Both riders demonstrated exceptional control and determination, adjusting their strategies in real time to try to secure the victory.

In the last lap, Márquez and Dovizioso were almost neck and neck, but it was Dovizioso who managed to make a decisive overtake in the final corners, dramatically securing the win.

Andrea Dovizioso's triumph at Motegi was not only a demonstration of his skill and bravery but also solidified his position as one of the main title contenders that season.

The 2017 Motegi race became an instant classic in MotoGP history due to the number of overtakes and the fierce competition between two of the world's best riders.

This Grand Prix is a perfect example of how adverse conditions can elevate the level of competition and drama in MotoGP, providing fans with an unforgettable experience.

The 2017 Motegi race is remembered as one of the most exciting and hard-fought, with a number of overtakes that underline the intensity and skill required to compete at the highest level in this sport.

60

MotoGP bikes must comply with a minimum weight regulation of 157 kg.

This regulation is implemented to ensure a level playing field among teams and to prevent the excessive use of ultra-light materials that could compromise rider safety.

The minimum weight includes the bike with all its components and fluids, except for the fuel.

Compliance with the minimum weight is a critical consideration in the design and development of MotoGP bikes.

Engineers and designers work hard to achieve the optimal balance between weight and performance, aiming to lighten the bikes as much as possible without falling below the regulatory limit.

The use of advanced materials such as carbon fiber, titanium, and lightweight alloys is common to reduce the weight of components without sacrificing structural integrity and safety.

Despite the minimum weight rule, there are slight variations in the weight of the bikes due to the different configurations and components used by each team.

Lighter bikes, which approach the 157 kg limit, tend to have advantages in terms of acceleration, handling, and fuel efficiency.

These advantages are especially noticeable on circuits with many corners and quick direction changes, where the bike's agility and responsiveness are crucial.

However, achieving a reduced weight is not the only goal.

The weight distribution and center of gravity of the bike also play a fundamental role in its performance.

Engineers adjust the placement of key components such as the engine, exhaust system, fuel tank, and other elements to optimize weight distribution and improve the bike's stability and traction.

A low and well-balanced center of gravity can significantly enhance the bike's handling and its ability to maintain traction in corners and during acceleration.

Regarding heavier bikes, although none can be below the minimum regulatory weight, differences in components and configurations can make some bikes marginally heavier than others.

Factors such as the type of chassis, engine configuration, and materials used can influence the final weight.

Teams work diligently to keep the weight as close as possible to the minimum allowed, but they must always consider stability, durability, and safety.

Weight management and distribution are constant challenges for MotoGP teams.

In addition to complying with minimum weight regulations, they must ensure that the bike can withstand the extreme stresses of racing without compromising rider safety.

This requires a combination of technological innovation, advanced materials, and meticulous design.

61

Honda is the most successful manufacturer in the history of MotoGP, amassing more constructors' championships and Grand Prix victories than any other team.

This success is largely due to its constant investment in research and development, as well as its ability to attract the best riders in the world.

Honda's history in MotoGP began in the 1960s when they entered the championship with a determined focus on innovation and high-quality engineering.

Since then, they have pioneered numerous technologies that have transformed competitive motorcycling.

Their commitment to research and development has allowed them to remain at the forefront of racing bike technology.

One key to Honda's success has been their ability to develop powerful and reliable engines.

Honda engines are known for their superior performance and durability, crucial factors in the demanding arena of MotoGP.

Additionally, Honda has invested significantly in the aerodynamics and electronics of their bikes, areas that have been fundamental to developing competitiveness on the track.

Honda has also been exceptionally effective in attracting and retaining elite riders.

Names like Mick Doohan, Valentino Rossi, Marc Márquez, and Casey Stoner have ridden for Honda, each contributing significantly to its legacy of success.

These riders have not only won multiple world championships but also provided crucial feedback for the continuous development of the bikes.

In terms of constructors' championships, Honda has amassed an impressive number of titles.

This achievement reflects not only the skill of their riders but also the team's ability to build and maintain bikes that are consistently competitive in a variety of conditions and circuits.

Grand Prix victories also highlight Honda's dominance in the sport.

They have won more races than any other manufacturer, a feat that underscores their ability to adapt and excel in an incredibly competitive and constantly evolving sport.

Each victory is the result of a collective effort involving engineers, mechanics, riders, and other team members working together to optimize the bike's performance.

Additionally, Honda has shown a remarkable ability to innovate and adapt to the changing rules of MotoGP.

62

The first MotoGP Grand Prix was held in 1949 at the Isle of Man TT circuit, known for being one of the most dangerous and challenging circuits in the world.

This event marked the beginning of the Motorcycle World Championship, organized by the International Motorcycling Federation (FIM), and set the standard for what would become one of the most prestigious and followed competitions in motorsport.

The Isle of Man TT, located in the Irish Sea, is famous for its mountain course that runs through closed public roads.

The circuit, over 60 kilometers long, features a combination of tight corners, fast straights, and elevation changes that test both the rider's skill and the bike's capability.

The nature of the circuit, with its narrow roads bordered by stone walls and buildings, makes it an extreme challenge in terms of safety and control.

In 1949, the championship included several categories based on the engine displacement of the bikes, and the inaugural race was a test of endurance and skill.

The categories were 500cc, 350cc, 250cc, and 125cc, along with a category for sidecars.

The 500cc race, the premier category, was won by British rider Freddie Frith, who rode a Velocette.

Frith dominated the race, showcasing a combination of speed and skill on a circuit that severely punished any mistake.

The success of this first race and the enthusiasm it generated firmly established the championship as an annual event.

The dangerous and technical nature of the Isle of Man TT circuit added an element of mystique and respect to the competition, attracting riders willing to push the limits of their skills and the capabilities of their machines.

The history of the Motorcycle World Championship has since been a constant evolution of technology, talent, and competition.

The introduction of new categories, the improvement in the safety of circuits and bikes, and the professionalization of the sport have led MotoGP to become a global platform for elite motorcycling.

Over the decades, the championship has seen the participation of iconic manufacturers like Honda, Yamaha, Ducati, Suzuki, and many others, each contributing to the development and innovation in the sport.

Legendary riders have emerged, setting records and creating unforgettable moments that have defined the history of MotoGP.

Although the inaugural race at the Isle of Man TT is no longer part of the MotoGP calendar due to increasing safety concerns, its legacy endures.

63

**Fergus Anderson is the oldest rider
to win a motorcycle Grand Prix.**

This remarkable achievement occurred when he won
the Spanish Grand Prix in 1953 at the age of 44 years
and 237 days.

Anderson, a British rider, is remembered not only
for this feat but also for his significant contributions
to the sport during his career.

Born on February 9, 1909, Fergus Anderson began his
motorcycling career competing in various categories
and quickly stood out for his skill and determination.

His professional career was notable for both its
longevity and his success in different engine
capacities, especially in the 350cc category.

The victory at the Spanish Grand Prix in 1953, held at
the Montjuïc circuit in Barcelona, was a testament to
his experience and prowess on the track.

Anderson was riding a Moto Guzzi, an Italian brand
that was a dominant force in motorcycling at the time.

His triumph in this race not only highlighted his talent
but also underscored the competitiveness and reliability
of Moto Guzzi bikes.

The race at Montjuïc was one of the most challenging
on the calendar, with its urban circuit requiring
precision and absolute control.

Anderson's ability to maintain concentration and performance at an age when most riders had already retired was impressive and demonstrated his exceptional physical and mental capacity.

Anderson's career was not limited to this single victory.

Throughout his trajectory, he won several Grand Prix races and established himself as one of the most respected riders of his era.

His technical knowledge and ability to adjust and improve the bikes also made him valuable to the teams he competed with.

Fergus Anderson's success at an advanced age remains an inspiration in the world of motorcycling.

His victory in the 1953 Spanish Grand Prix set a record that still stands, highlighting the possibility that skill and experience can surpass youth and sheer speed in motorsport.

64

The 2015 Grand Prix of the Valencian Community set a record attendance with over 110,000 spectators present.

This event was especially significant as it marked the culmination of one of the most exciting and controversial seasons in MotoGP history.

Fans gathered at the Circuit Ricardo Tormo to witness the final battle for the world championship between Jorge Lorenzo and Valentino Rossi.

Jorge Lorenzo, a rider for the Movistar Yamaha team, arrived in Valencia with the opportunity to win his fifth world title and his third in the MotoGP category.

The tension was palpable, as the season had been filled with intense competition and controversies, particularly between Lorenzo, Rossi, and Marc Márquez.

The Grand Prix of Valencia would not only be decisive for the championship but was also charged with expectations due to the events that had unfolded during the year.

The race was an electrifying spectacle.

Jorge Lorenzo started from pole position and led the race from start to finish, showcasing impeccable riding under immense pressure.

Valentino Rossi, who had to start from the last position on the grid due to a penalty imposed after a controversial incident at the Malaysian Grand Prix with Marc Márquez, made an impressive comeback but it wasn't enough to catch Lorenzo.

Lorenzo's victory in Valencia secured him the world championship, making him the 2015 MotoGP champion.

The atmosphere at the circuit was electrifying, with fans cheering and celebrating Lorenzo's achievement.

65

Leslie Graham was the first world champion of the premier class of MotoGP, then known as 500cc, in 1949.

Graham, a British rider, marked the beginning of the sport's history with his remarkable achievement.

Born on September 14, 1911, in Wallasey, Cheshire, England, Leslie Graham began his motorcycling career before World War II and returned to competitions after the conflict.

In 1949, the International Motorcycling Federation (FIM) established the Motorcycle World Championship, which included several categories based on the engine displacement of the bikes, with the 500cc category being the primary and most prestigious.

Graham competed that year on an AJS bike, a British motorcycle brand with a strong reputation in racing at the time.

The 1949 season consisted of six Grand Prix races held at various European circuits.

Graham demonstrated his skill and consistency throughout the season, facing high-level competitors.

He won two of the six races, the Swiss Grand Prix and the Ulster Grand Prix, and secured important points in the other races, allowing him to accumulate the most points in the overall standings.

Leslie Graham's victory in the inaugural 500cc championship set a standard for future competitors and marked the beginning of an era of excellence in competitive motorcycling.

His success was the result of his talent as a rider, his determination, and his team's ability to prepare a competitive bike for each race.

Graham continued to compete in the Motorcycle World Championship in the following years and remained a prominent figure in the sport.

However, his career was tragically cut short in 1953 when he died in an accident during the Isle of Man TT, one of the most dangerous and challenging races on the calendar.

The legacy of Leslie Graham endures in the history of MotoGP.

His achievement as the first world champion of the premier class is a significant milestone that recalls the early days of the championship and the pioneering spirit of the sport's early years.

Graham was not only an exceptional rider but also an inspiration for future generations of riders aspiring to achieve greatness in the sport.

66

Tadayuki Okada was the first Asian rider to win a MotoGP race, achieving this feat at the Japanese Grand Prix in Suzuka in 1997.

This achievement was significant not only for Okada but also for Asian motorcycling, as it put riders from the region on the map of international motorcycling.

Tadayuki Okada, born on February 13, 1967, in Kurashiki, Japan, began his motorcycling career in Japanese national categories before making the leap to the international scene.

His talent and skills soon caught the attention of European teams, and in 1994 he joined the World Championship in the 250cc category, competing for Honda.

After several successful seasons in 250cc, Okada was promoted to the 500cc category (now known as MotoGP) in 1996, riding for the Repsol Honda team.

In his first year in the premier class, he showed solid performance, establishing himself as one of the promising riders in the championship.

The historic moment came in 1997 during the Japanese Grand Prix at Suzuka, a challenging and technical circuit well known to Japanese riders.

Okada, with the support of his team and leveraging his knowledge of the circuit, competed exceptionally well.

The race was intense, with several riders battling for the win, but Okada managed to maintain the calm and consistency needed to cross the finish line in first place.

This victory was not only a personal milestone for Tadayuki Okada but also a significant breakthrough for Asian motorcycling.

Before this achievement, no Asian rider had won a race in the premier category of the Motorcycle World Championship.

Okada's victory inspired many young riders in Asia and demonstrated that riders from the region could compete and succeed at the highest level of the sport.

Okada's career continued successfully, including several additional wins and podiums.

67

The rider's weight can significantly influence the performance of the motorcycle.

Lighter riders typically benefit from better acceleration and handling due to the lower total mass that the bike needs to move and control.

This weight reduction allows the bike to accelerate more quickly and change direction more agilely, which is especially beneficial on circuits with many curves and quick direction changes.

On the other hand, heavier riders may have certain advantages in terms of stability and traction.

The additional weight can help keep the bike's wheels more firmly on the ground, which can be beneficial at high speeds and in situations where extra traction is needed, such as hard braking and exiting corners.

This extra weight can provide a lower center of gravity and stabilize the bike, making it more predictable and manageable in certain situations.

Weight management is a critical consideration for MotoGP teams and riders.

Teams work meticulously to optimize the bike's weight and its distribution.

Every component of the bike is designed and manufactured to be as light as possible without compromising safety and durability.

This includes the use of advanced materials such as carbon fiber, titanium, and lightweight alloys.

Riders also pay close attention to their own weight and physical condition.

Staying fit and at an optimal weight is part of every rider's training regimen.

Riders often work with nutritionists and physical trainers to ensure they are in the best possible shape, maintaining a proper balance between strength, endurance, and body weight.

In addition to weight optimization, weight distribution is equally important.

The way weight is distributed between the front and rear of the bike can significantly affect its handling and performance.

Engineers adjust the position of key components such as the engine, exhaust system, and fuel tank to achieve optimal weight distribution.

Riders also adjust their position on the bike during the race to better manage weight distribution, moving forward or backward as needed.

The combination of the bike and the rider as an integrated system is crucial for success in MotoGP.

The interaction between the bike's weight and the rider's weight can affect aspects such as tire wear, fuel efficiency, and the ability to maintain a consistent pace throughout the race.

68

The fastest lap in MotoGP history was recorded by Jorge Lorenzo at the Mugello Circuit in 2018, with a time of 1:46.208.

This impressive achievement not only highlights Lorenzo's skill and precision as a rider but also the technical excellence and superior performance of the bike he was riding.

The Mugello Circuit, located in the Tuscany region of Italy, is known for its challenging and varied layout, which includes a combination of long straights, fast and technical corners, and elevation changes.

These characteristics make the circuit a true test for riders and their machines, requiring a combination of speed, control, and technical prowess.

Jorge Lorenzo's record lap in 2018 was achieved during the qualifying session for the Italian Grand Prix.

Riding a Ducati, Lorenzo demonstrated exceptional ability to maximize his bike's performance in every section of the circuit.

The precision with which he took the corners, the acceleration on the straights, and the handling of elevation changes were key factors in achieving this record time.

The time of 1:46.208 reflects not only the top speed achieved on the straights but also the efficiency with which Lorenzo and his bike were able to maintain high speed through the corners and manage traction and stability throughout the lap.

This type of performance requires a perfect balance between the rider and the machine, as well as meticulous bike setup to suit the specific conditions of the Mugello circuit.

Lorenzo's achievement at Mugello is a testament to his talent as one of the best MotoGP riders of his generation.

Throughout his career, Lorenzo has been known for his smooth and precise riding style, as well as his ability to maintain a consistent and fast pace throughout the race.

These attributes were clearly evident in his record lap.

In addition to the rider's skill, the fastest lap also highlights the importance of technology and engineering in MotoGP.

69

Traction control was introduced in MotoGP in the early 2000s and has had a significant impact on the sport.

This electronic system helps prevent wheel spin during acceleration, especially in low-traction conditions such as corners or wet surfaces.

Its implementation has allowed riders to be more aggressive in acceleration, improving lap times and increasing safety on the track.

Traction control works by constantly monitoring wheel speeds and adjusting the engine's power delivery to prevent the rear wheels from losing grip.

When slippage is detected, the system temporarily reduces power to restore traction.

This allows riders to maintain optimal acceleration without worrying about losing control, especially when exiting corners where power application is critical.

The introduction of traction control has transformed the way riders approach acceleration and bike handling.

Before its implementation, riders had to be extremely careful with the throttle to avoid wheel slip, limiting their ability to accelerate aggressively.

With traction control, riders can trust the system to manage power delivery, allowing them to focus more on the racing line and strategy.

This technology has contributed to improved lap times, as riders can accelerate earlier and more forcefully when exiting corners.

The ability to apply more power in a controlled manner has helped reduce lap times and increase competitiveness.

Additionally, traction control has allowed engineers to optimize other aspects of the bike, knowing that power delivery will be effectively managed by the system.

In terms of safety, traction control has been a significant advancement. By reducing the risk of slipping and crashes due to loss of traction, it has helped protect riders in challenging conditions.

This is especially important on wet or slippery surfaces, where manual throttle control can be extremely challenging.

The technology provides an additional layer of safety, allowing riders to push the limits of their bikes with greater confidence.

The impact of traction control has also been seen in the evolution of race strategies and tire management.

Riders and teams can adjust traction control levels to suit different track conditions and riding styles.

This flexibility allows for more precise tire management, optimizing their performance and durability during the race.

Despite its advantages, traction control has been a subject of debate.

Some purists argue that the technology can reduce the skill required by riders, as part of the challenge of managing power is transferred to the electronic system.

Nonetheless, most recognize that the combination of rider talent and advanced technology is what drives progress in MotoGP.

70

**Kenny Roberts was the first American
rider to win a MotoGP world title in 1978.**

His victory not only marked an important milestone in
the history of motorcycling but also transformed the
sport with his innovative riding style and professional
approach.

Born on December 31, 1951, in Modesto, California,
Roberts was already a prominent figure in motocross
and dirt track competitions in the United States before
making his debut on the world stage.

Roberts joined the Motorcycle World Championship in
the 500cc category (now known as MotoGP) in 1978,
competing for the Yamaha team.

From his first season, he demonstrated exceptional
skill and adaptability, quickly adjusting to the European
circuits and the demands of the world championship.

His meticulous and professional approach to the
sport, which included rigorous physical and mental
preparation, set new standards for MotoGP riders.

Roberts' riding style was revolutionary.

He introduced the technique of "sliding" the bike through
corners, controlling the rear wheel's drift to maintain
higher speed and stability.

This technique, combined with his aggression and
precision on the track, allowed him to dominate races
and outpace many of his rivals.

His ability to understand and improve the bike's performance was also fundamental to his success.

The 1978 season was spectacular for Roberts.

He won four Grand Prix races and accumulated crucial points in several other races, securing the world championship at the end of the season.

His victory broke the dominance of European riders and proved that American riders could compete and triumph at the highest level of world motorcycling.

Roberts' impact on the sport was profound and lasting.

His success inspired a new generation of American riders, such as Eddie Lawson, Wayne Rainey, and Kevin Schwantz, who also became world champions in the following years.

Moreover, his professional approach and dedication to training and preparation set a new standard that other riders would follow.

Roberts continued his career in MotoGP, winning two more consecutive world titles in 1979 and 1980, cementing his place as a legend of the sport.

After retiring as a rider, he continued to influence motorcycling as a team owner and mentor to young riders.

71

**Until the early 2000s, MotoGP
bikes used 2-stroke engines.**

These engines were known for their high power and
acceleration, making them extremely fast and exciting
to watch on the track.

The nature of 2-stroke engines allowed them to reach high
revolutions per minute (RPM) and deliver explosive power,
resulting in impressive acceleration. However, these engines
also presented several challenges.

They were less reliable, with a higher tendency for
mechanical failures due to the high stresses and
temperatures they endured.

Additionally, 2-stroke engines were more difficult to handle,
as their abrupt power delivery could make the bikes less
predictable and harder to control, especially in corners.

The era of 2-stroke engines was a time of great innovation
and fierce competition in MotoGP.

Legendary riders such as Mick Doohan, Wayne Rainey,
and Kevin Schwantz stood out during this period,
demonstrating exceptional skills in handling 2-stroke
bikes and winning world championships.

The races were intensely competitive and thrilling,
with frequent position changes and daring maneuvers.

In 2002, MotoGP introduced 4-stroke engines, replacing
the 2-stroke engines that had been the standard.

This transition marked a significant change in the dynamics
of the sport.

Four-stroke engines are more efficient and produce more power in a more controlled manner.

Unlike two-stroke engines, four-stroke engines offer smoother and more linear power delivery, making the bikes easier to handle and improving stability.

Four-stroke engines are also more reliable and durable, reducing the frequency of mechanical failures and allowing riders and teams to focus more on strategy and on-track performance.

These engines operate at lower RPMs compared to two-stroke engines but compensate for this difference with greater torque and better fuel management, resulting in overall superior efficiency.

The introduction of four-stroke engines significantly changed the dynamics of MotoGP racing.

The bikes became faster and more consistent, and teams could explore new strategies and setups to optimize performance.

This change also led to accelerated development of technology and electronics in the bikes, including advanced traction control systems, electronic suspension, and real-time telemetry.

The impact of four-stroke engines was reflected in the evolution of lap times and the competitiveness of the championship.

Riders like Valentino Rossi, Marc Márquez, and Jorge Lorenzo took advantage of the new engines to dominate on the track and set new records.

MotoGP races became an even more impressive spectacle, with bikes that combined raw power, precise handling, and advanced technology to deliver exceptional performance.

72

The Malaysian Grand Prix at Sepang is famous for its sudden and heavy rain showers, and the 2012 edition is a prominent example of how weather can significantly impact MotoGP races.

Sepang, known for its tropical and humid climate, often presents unpredictable weather conditions that can dramatically transform a race in a matter of minutes.

In 2012, the Malaysian Grand Prix witnessed one of the rainiest races in MotoGP history.

The race began under cloudy skies, but the conditions quickly worsened.

Heavy rain started shortly after the beginning, making the track extremely slippery and dangerous for the riders.

Visibility was drastically reduced, and water puddles began to form on the circuit, increasing the risk of aquaplaning and crashes.

As the conditions worsened, several riders began to struggle to maintain control of their bikes.

Crashes and slides became more frequent, and rider safety became an increasing concern.

The intensity of the rain increased so much that the race direction decided to wave the red flag, stopping the race for safety reasons.

The decision to stop the race was made after completing 13 of the scheduled 20 laps.

At that moment, Dani Pedrosa was leading the race, followed by Jorge Lorenzo and Casey Stoner.

With the race halted and the weather conditions preventing a restart, the results were declared based on the positions at the end of lap 13.

This event clearly demonstrated how weather can significantly impact MotoGP races.

Heavy rain not only affects visibility and traction but can also endanger rider safety.

The ability of the organizers to make quick decisions and ensure safety is crucial in such situations.

73

The Tech3 team is widely recognized as one of the most successful satellite teams in MotoGP history.

Throughout its trajectory, Tech3 has been a satellite team for Yamaha and, more recently, for KTM.

Their success is largely due to their ability to develop and nurture future champions, as well as their numerous podiums and standout performances in the premier class of motorcycle racing.

Founded by Hervé Poncharal, Tech3 began its journey in the Motorcycle World Championship in the 250cc category before moving up to the premier class in 2001.

Their partnership with Yamaha started in 2001, and for nearly two decades, Tech3 became the go-to satellite team for the Japanese brand.

The collaboration between Tech3 and Yamaha resulted in numerous successes, both in terms of rider development and on-track results.

One of the most notable moments for Tech3 was the 2008 season, when British rider James Toseland and American rider Colin Edwards achieved several podiums.

Edwards, in particular, was a key figure for the team, securing multiple podiums and helping to solidify Tech3's reputation as a competitive team capable of challenging factory teams.

Another standout rider for Tech3 was Cal Crutchlow.

The Brit, known for his aggression and determination, achieved several podiums during his time with the team, cementing his reputation as one of the most talented riders on the grid.

Crutchlow was fundamental for Tech3, demonstrating that the team could compete at the highest level and challenge factory teams on several occasions.

The team also played a crucial role in the development of Johann Zarco.

The French rider, who won the Moto2 title in 2015 and 2016, joined Tech3 in 2017 and quickly showed his potential in the premier class.

Zarco achieved several podiums and became one of the most impressive rookies in recent MotoGP history.

His success with Tech3 highlighted the team's ability to identify and develop emerging talent.

In 2019, Tech3 switched its alliance from Yamaha to KTM, becoming the satellite team for the Austrian brand.

This new partnership brought new challenges and opportunities.

Under the KTM banner, Tech3 continued to demonstrate its ability to compete and achieve standout results.

In 2020, Miguel Oliveira secured two victories for the team, at the Styrian Grand Prix and the Portuguese Grand Prix, marking a significant milestone in Tech3's history and confirming its status as one of the most successful satellite teams.

In addition to their on-track successes, Tech3 has been instrumental in the training and development of many riders who later achieved success with factory teams.

The combination of effective management, a focus on talent development, and the ability to adapt to different manufacturers has been key to the team's sustained success.

74

Loris Capirossi holds the record as the youngest rider to win a race in the premier class of MotoGP, having achieved this feat at the age of 17 years and 165 days in 1990.

This record underscores the presence and impact of young talent in the championship, which has been a distinctive feature of MotoGP over the years.

Loris Capirossi, born on April 4, 1973, in Castel San Pietro Terme, Italy, debuted in the Motorcycle World Championship at a very young age.

In 1990, he competed in the 125cc category, where he quickly demonstrated his potential by winning the British Grand Prix at Donington Park.

His victory made him the youngest winner of a race in the premier class, a feat that has yet to be surpassed.

Capirossi's early success not only highlighted his innate talent but also marked the beginning of a long and successful career in motorcycling.

After his victory in 125cc, he continued to progress and win championships.

In 1990 and 1991, he won the 125cc World Championship, cementing his reputation as one of the most promising riders of his generation.

Throughout his career, Capirossi competed in various categories, including 250cc and 500cc/MotoGP, achieving multiple victories and podiums.

His ability to adapt to different bikes and race conditions allowed him to remain competitive for over two decades in the sport.

Capirossi is known for his aggression and determination on the track, as well as his ability to ride at the highest level.

Capirossi's record for precocity has inspired many young riders to pursue their dreams in MotoGP.

His success demonstrated that age is not a barrier to talent and that young riders can compete and win against the best in the world.

This achievement has contributed to the trend in MotoGP of promoting and developing young talent, allowing them to enter the championship at increasingly younger ages.

In addition to Capirossi, other young riders have also left their mark on the history of MotoGP.

Riders like Marc Márquez and Valentino Rossi began their careers in the championship at a young age and quickly established themselves as title contenders.

These riders have followed the path paved by Capirossi, showing that the combination of talent, determination, and proper support can lead to success at an early age.

75

Valentino Rossi is famous for his number 46, which he has used throughout his entire MotoGP career and has become an icon in the world of motorcycling.

This number holds personal and emotional significance for Rossi, as it was used by his father, Graziano Rossi, also a motorcycle racer, during his racing days.

Valentino decided to keep the number 46 as a tribute to his father, and over time, this number has become synonymous with his success and legacy in the sport.

Graziano Rossi, born on March 14, 1954, was a prominent motorcycle racer in the 1970s.

He competed in various categories, including 250cc and 500cc, achieving several podiums and victories during his career.

Graziano used the number 46 on his bikes, and this number became part of the Rossi family's identity in motorcycling.

When Valentino Rossi began his motorcycling career, he chose to adopt the number 46 in honor of his father.

This gesture not only reflected his admiration for Graziano but also established a symbolic link between generations.

From his early days in youth competitions to his rise to the top categories of the Motorcycle World Championship, Rossi has kept the number 46 on all his bikes.

The number 46 quickly became a symbol of Valentino Rossi's presence and dominance in MotoGP.

His bold riding style, charisma, and consistent success contributed to the number 46 being associated with excellence in motorcycling.

Rossi won his first world championship in the 125cc category in 1997, followed by titles in 250cc and finally in the premier class of 500cc/MotoGP.

Throughout his career, Valentino Rossi has amassed nine world championships, solidifying his status as one of the greatest riders of all time.

Each victory and each championship won with the number 46 has reinforced his legacy and made the number synonymous with greatness in the sport.

MotoGP fans around the world recognize and celebrate the number 46, which has appeared on a wide range of merchandise, from t-shirts and hats to flags and stickers.

The impact of the number 46 transcends the racetrack. It has influenced popular culture and become a symbol of inspiration for young riders and motorcycle enthusiasts.

Valentino Rossi's decision to keep the number 46 has created a deep connection with his fans, who see it as a symbol of dedication, passion, and family heritage.

76

Chassis configurations in MotoGP are a crucial element for the handling and overall performance of the bike.

Engineers work meticulously to adjust the chassis, seeking a perfect balance between rigidity and flexibility.

This balance is fundamental for riders to handle corners with precision and stability, maximize traction, and optimize the bike's response in different racing conditions.

The chassis of a MotoGP bike is composed of several key components, including the main frame, the swingarm, and the subframe.

Each of these components can be adjusted to modify the bike's handling characteristics.

The main frame is the backbone of the bike, connecting all the main components such as the engine, the front and rear suspension, and the steering system.

The rigidity of the frame is crucial for the bike's handling.

A frame that is too rigid can offer great precision in fast corners but may be less forgiving on uneven surfaces, transmitting all vibrations to the rider.

On the other hand, a more flexible frame can better absorb irregularities in the terrain, providing a more comfortable ride but less precision in fast corners.

The swingarm is the component that connects the rear wheel to the bike and allows the movement of the rear suspension.

Adjusting the length and rigidity of the swingarm can significantly change the bike's behavior in acceleration and cornering.

A longer swingarm can provide greater stability on straights and better traction when exiting corners, while a shorter one can make the bike more agile and easier to turn.

The subframe, which supports the seat and other rear parts of the bike, also plays a role in weight distribution and overall chassis rigidity.

Adjusting the subframe can influence the bike's center of gravity, affecting how it behaves in different riding situations.

Engineers also adjust the chassis geometry, which includes parameters such as the fork rake angle, trail, and wheelbase.

These adjustments fine-tune how the bike responds to steering and how stable it remains at high speeds.

A steeper rake angle can make the bike more agile, while a smaller angle can increase stability on straights.

The material of the chassis is also an important consideration.

MotoGP chassis are typically made of aluminum or carbon fiber.

Aluminum offers a good balance between rigidity and weight, while carbon fiber, though more expensive, provides superior rigidity and is lighter, thus improving the bike's overall performance.

Suspension is another critical component that interacts with the chassis.

Engineers adjust the stiffness of the front and rear shocks, as well as the spring preload, compression, and rebound damping, to optimize the bike's handling on different types of tracks and under various weather conditions.

A well-adjusted suspension can improve traction and stability, allowing riders to brake later and accelerate earlier when exiting corners.

The process of adjusting the chassis is continuous and relies on extensive testing and rider feedback.

During practice and qualifying sessions, riders provide detailed information on how the bike feels in different parts of the circuit.

Engineers use this information to make precise adjustments, constantly seeking to improve the bike's performance.

77

The 2018 French Grand Prix at Le Mans is known for being one of the races with the most crashes in recent MotoGP history, mainly due to the wet track conditions.

The challenging weather presented a significant challenge for the riders, who had to demonstrate their skill and dexterity to handle the extreme situation.

During this Grand Prix, the rain began to fall just before the race, leading to a wet and slippery track.

These conditions are especially difficult at Le Mans, a circuit known for its mix of fast and slow corners, as well as its particular asphalt that can become extremely treacherous when wet.

The combination of rain and the characteristics of the circuit resulted in numerous crashes throughout the race.

The lack of proper traction and tricky braking areas made it necessary for the riders to be extremely cautious, but despite their best efforts, many encountered difficulties.

Crashes occurred at various points around the circuit, highlighting how difficult it was to keep the bike under control in those conditions.

Despite the high number of crashes, the riders demonstrated an impressive level of skill and determination.

Many of them managed to recover from incidents and continue racing, showing great resilience and the ability to quickly adapt to the changing track conditions.

Marc Márquez, who eventually won the race, showcased remarkable mastery in handling the adverse conditions.

His ability to find the right balance between speed and caution allowed him to avoid crashes and maintain a consistent pace, which was key to his victory.

Márquez demonstrated why he is considered one of the greatest riders of all time, managing the pressure and difficult conditions with extraordinary skill.

The 2018 Le Mans race was notable not only for the number of crashes but also for the strategy and preparation of the teams and riders.

Tire choice was crucial, with many riders opting for intermediate or wet compounds to better handle the lack of traction.

Engineers and mechanics worked tirelessly to adjust the bike setups, aiming to maximize stability and control on the wet track.

In addition to the crashes, the race was also a spectacle of overtakes and tactical maneuvers.

The riders had to constantly adapt to the changing conditions, leading to intense and exciting competition.

The riders' ability to make overtakes in such adverse conditions highlighted their incredible skill and courage.

78

**Marc Márquez holds the record for the most points
in a MotoGP season, with 420 points obtained in 2019.**

This nearly perfect season is an impressive display of
his dominance and consistency in the premier class of
motorcycle racing.

During this season, Márquez achieved 12 victories and 6 second-
place finishes in a total of 19 races, highlighting his ability to stay
at the top in almost every competition.

The 2019 MotoGP season was exceptional for Márquez and his
team, Repsol Honda.

From the beginning, Márquez showed incredible form, starting with
a dominant victory in the Argentine Grand Prix, the second race
of the calendar.

This victory set the tone for the rest of the season, as Márquez
continued to accumulate points with astonishing regularity.

One of the highlights of the season was his ability to handle
different conditions and challenges on various circuits around
the world.

Márquez demonstrated exceptional adaptability, winning on
technical circuits like Sachsenring and high-speed tracks
like Phillip Island.

His ability to find the limit and maintain control, even in difficult
conditions, was key to his success.

In addition to his 12 victories, Márquez finished in second place
6 times, demonstrating his consistency and ability to maximize
points even when not winning.

His worst result of the season was a single retirement, highlighting
his remarkable consistency.

This ability to consistently finish on the podium allowed him to quickly accumulate points and build an insurmountable lead in the championship.

The 2019 season was also notable for the thrilling battles Márquez fought with other elite riders such as Andrea Dovizioso, Fabio Quartararo, and Maverick Viñales.

These competitions not only highlighted his ability to compete under pressure but also his capacity to execute precise and strategic overtaking maneuvers at crucial moments.

Márquez's performance in 2019 not only secured him the world title but also cemented his position as one of the greatest riders in MotoGP history.

His ability to combine speed, precision, and consistency throughout such a demanding season is a testament to his talent and dedication.

The contribution of his team, Repsol Honda, was also fundamental.

The Honda RC213V was an exceptionally competitive machine in 2019, and the collaboration between Márquez and his team of engineers and mechanics allowed for optimal performance in every race.

Communication and understanding within the team were key to adjusting the bike to the specific needs of each circuit and race condition.

79

Some MotoGP teams have begun using artificial intelligence (AI) and machine learning to analyze large volumes of data and predict bike performance.

These advanced technologies are revolutionizing the way teams approach race preparation and execution, significantly improving the precision of adjustments and race strategy.

The incorporation of AI in MotoGP involves using advanced algorithms to process and analyze data collected from various sources, such as sensors installed on the bikes that measure parameters like speed, acceleration, tire temperature, G-forces, and many other factors.

This data is essential for understanding how the bike behaves under different conditions and how adjustments can affect its performance.

One key application of AI in MotoGP is optimizing bike setup.

Engineers use machine learning algorithms to identify patterns in historical and current data, allowing them to predict how changes in setup can influence performance.

For example, they can adjust suspension, chassis geometry, weight distribution, and other critical parameters to maximize traction, stability, and handling on different tracks and under various weather conditions.

Additionally, AI enables the simulation of race scenarios, where the outcomes of different strategies can be predicted.

Teams can use predictive models to anticipate how races will develop based on various variables such as weather, track conditions, and tire behavior.

This allows teams to plan their strategies more effectively, optimizing pit stop timing, tire selection, and overtaking tactics.

AI is also used to analyze rider performance.

By evaluating biometric data and riding patterns, teams can identify areas where riders can improve.

For example, they can detect inconsistencies in lines, braking, or acceleration and provide specific feedback to help riders refine their technique and improve their on-track performance.

Another area where AI is making a difference is in predictive maintenance.

By continuously monitoring the condition of bike components, AI algorithms can predict when failures or wear are likely to occur, allowing teams to perform preventive maintenance before these issues become critical during a race.

The use of artificial intelligence in MotoGP not only enhances performance and strategy but also contributes to safety.

By predicting potentially hazardous conditions and adjusting bike setup accordingly, teams can reduce the risk of accidents and improve overall rider safety.

80

MotoGP has introduced the MotoE category, which uses electric bikes instead of traditional internal combustion engine bikes.

This new category, officially known as the FIM Enel MotoE World Cup, was launched in 2019 with the goal of promoting sustainability and technological innovation in the sport of motorcycling.

MotoE bikes are designed to be more environmentally friendly, eliminating carbon emissions and reducing the environmental footprint of racing.

This initiative aligns with global trends toward electrification and sustainability in the transportation industry.

By incorporating electric bikes, MotoGP is not only showing its commitment to the environment but also driving the development of advanced technologies that could benefit street bikes in the future.

Despite being quieter than traditional MotoGP bikes, MotoE bikes offer impressive performance.

Equipped with powerful electric motors and high-capacity batteries, these bikes can reach top speeds close to those of internal combustion engine bikes.

Acceleration is particularly notable due to the instant torque that electric motors can provide.

Riders have praised the responsiveness and power delivery of the MotoE bikes, which offer a unique and thrilling riding experience.

The MotoE category has been well received by motorcycle enthusiasts, who appreciate both the technological innovation and the focus on sustainability.

MotoE races, although shorter in duration due to current battery limitations, are equally exciting and competitive.

Riders in this category compete fiercely, demonstrating that electric bikes can provide a spectacle as thrilling as their internal combustion counterparts.

The MotoE championship has also served as a testing ground for new technologies.

Developments in batteries, energy management systems, and lightweight materials are being driven by the demands of racing.

These advances not only benefit the racing bikes but can also influence the consumer electric vehicle market, accelerating the adoption of more efficient and sustainable technologies.

MotoE has attracted a mix of experienced riders and young talents, some of whom have competed in other MotoGP categories.

This diversity on the starting grid has contributed to the competitiveness and variety of the championship.

81

The braking distances in MotoGP are impressive due to the bikes' ability to decelerate quickly thanks to their advanced carbon brake systems.

These bikes can decelerate from 300 km/h to 100 km/h in less than 5 seconds, resulting in an extremely short braking distance.

This ability to brake late and precisely is a crucial skill for riders and one of the areas where positions can be gained or lost during races.

The carbon brakes used in MotoGP are among the most advanced technologies in motorsport.

These brakes offer several advantages over traditional steel brakes, including greater heat resistance, lower weight, and better braking capacity.

Heat resistance is particularly important in MotoGP races, where the brakes can reach extremely high temperatures due to repeated heavy braking on each lap.

Carbon brakes maintain their performance even at high temperatures, allowing riders to brake consistently and precisely throughout the race.

The ability of MotoGP bikes to decelerate from 300 km/h to 100 km/h in less than 5 seconds is due not only to the quality of the brakes but also to the design of the chassis and aerodynamics of the bike.

During intense braking, riders experience significant G-forces, often exceeding 1.5 Gs.

Weight distribution, chassis rigidity, and suspension setup play crucial roles in the bike's stability during these extreme braking maneuvers.

The ability to brake late and precisely is one of the distinguishing characteristics of the best riders.

Riders must accurately judge the exact braking point to maximize speed on the straights and minimize time in the corners, requiring a combination of instinct, experience, and a deep understanding of the bike and the circuit.

The braking technique includes modulating the brake to avoid wheel lockup, which could result in a loss of control and a potential crash.

Engineers adjust the bike's setup to optimize braking performance.

This includes suspension adjustments to handle the weight transfer to the front wheel during braking and brake settings to ensure precise and powerful response.

MotoGP braking systems also incorporate advanced technology such as ABS (anti-lock braking system) in a form adapted for racing, which helps prevent wheel lockup during extreme braking.

The ability to brake late and precisely has a significant impact on MotoGP races.

Overtakes often occur in braking zones, where riders attempt to out-brake their rivals by braking later and maintaining control in the corners.

A rider's ability to handle these situations successfully can be the difference between gaining or losing a position, or even winning or losing a race.

A typical example of extreme deceleration in MotoGP can be seen at circuits like the Mugello Circuit or the Circuit de Barcelona-Catalunya, where bikes reach speeds over 300 km/h on the straights before braking sharply for tight corners.

In these cases, riders must apply a great amount of force to the brakes, reducing speed over a very short distance while maintaining control of the bike.

Printed in Great Britain
by Amazon

49673010R00086